The BOYS' GUIDE to DRAWING

REVISED AND UPDATED EDITION

by **Clara Cella** and **Aaron Sautter**

illustrated by **S. Altmann, Charles Barnett III, Brian Bascle, Steve Erwin, Jason Knudson, Bob Lentz, Cynthia Martin,** and **Jon Westwood**

CAPSTONE PRESS
a capstone imprint

TABLE OF CONTENTS

MANGA WARRIORS

VEHICLES

OTHER COOL STUFF

HELLO, ARTIST!

WELCOME TO YOUR PRIVATE ART CLASS! Whether you're a notebook doodler or an artist with a capital "A," you'll find tons of projects to love in here. What would you like to draw first? An alien that's part frog, part octopus? A fighter jet faster than the speed of sound? How about a sword-carrying manga warrior or a family of superheroes? A great white shark or a T-rex?

After you've picked your project, follow the simple step-by-step instructions. Some projects and steps are trickier than others. Take your time, and practice, practice, practice. Be sure to check the little idea bubbles for ways to take your drawings in new directions and

MAKE THEM YOUR OWN!

TOOLS AND SUPPLIES

Before you begin your drawing projects,
gather the following tools and supplies:

PAPER
Any type of blank, unlined paper will do.

PENCILS
Pencils are the easiest to use.
Make sure you have plenty of them.

SHARPENER
You'll need clean lines, so keep
a pencil sharpener close by.

ERASER
Pencil erasers wear out very quickly.
Get a rubber or kneaded eraser.

DARK PEN/MARKER
When your drawing is finished, you can
trace over it with a black ink pen or a thin
felt-tip marker. The dark lines will really
make your work pop.

COLORED PENCILS
If you decide to color your drawings,
colored pencils usually work best.

OUTER SPACE

GREETINGS FROM PLANET OOLOC . . .
the Pluponian Nebula . . . and the Blixby Galaxy!
The 17 creatures and alien vehicles in this section
have traveled a great distance to be here. Not to
eat you or take you prisoner (don't worry!), but
to meet you and ask you to draw their portraits.

You've already drawn the stuff you see here on
Earth. Time to suit up and blast into outer space.
In no time at all, you'll have countless pages of
OUT-OF-THIS-WORLD AWESOME!

VOGGLES

Voggles are some of the weirdest aliens you'll ever see. Their special eye antennae let each Voggle see what all other Voggles see. This makes Voggles the best security guards around for the Helix Galactic Bank.

STEP 1

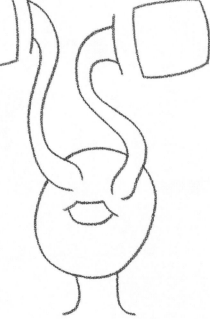

STEP 2

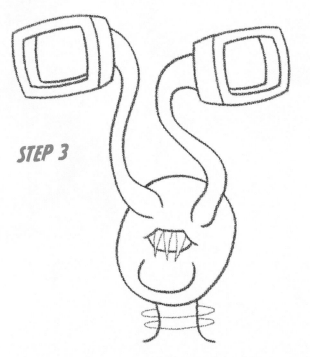

STEP 3

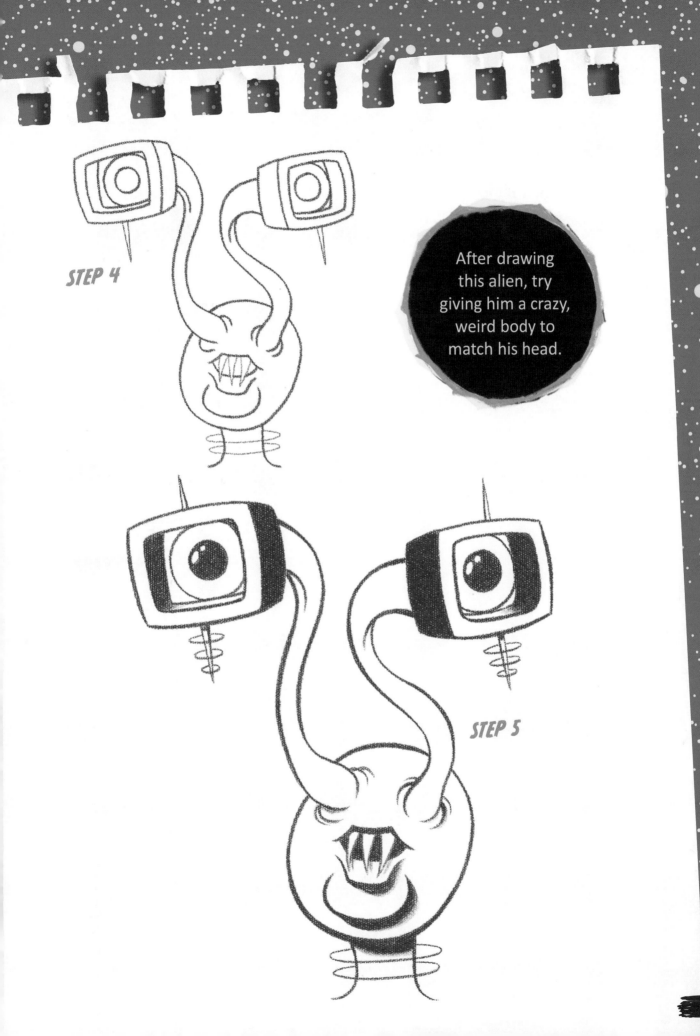

STEP 4

After drawing this alien, try giving him a crazy, weird body to match his head.

STEP 5

SKRAWKS

The Skrawk people have been involved in galactic politics for hundreds of years. They think every person's opinion is important. Skrawks who aren't involved with politics usually work as lawyers or for the Galactic Peace Corps.

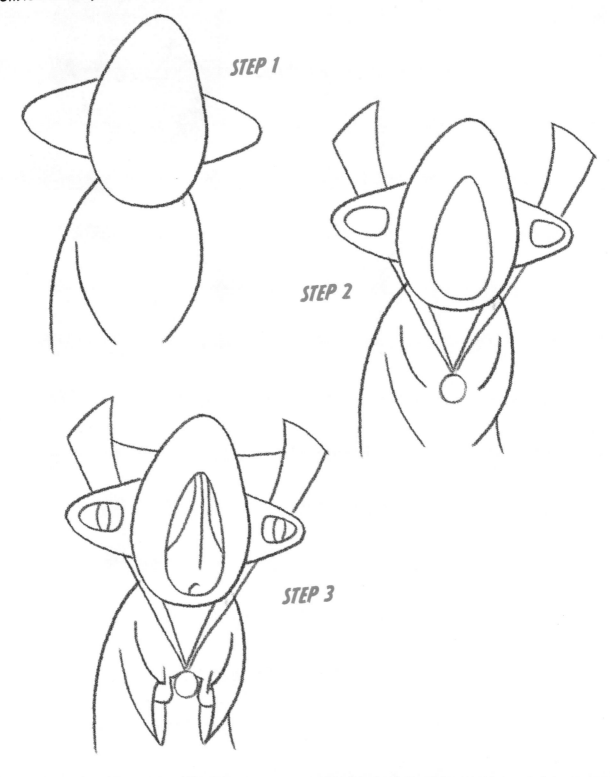

STEP 1

STEP 2

STEP 3

STEP 4

Now give your Skrawk a new suit or a snazzy Peace Corps uniform.

STEP 5

THE GIANT BLORP

If you're ever on the planet Tantil-3, watch out for the Giant Blorp! At first it seems like a gentle snail-like creature. But don't get too close! If the Blorp smells you, it'll grab you with its sticky tongue tentacles and gobble you up for breakfast!

STEP 1

STEP 2

STEP 3

STEP 4

After drawing this picture, give the Giant Blorp even more tongue tentacles.

STEP 5

SNALIDS

Anelid Prime is home to a dangerous alien race. Snalids are slippery creatures with mouths full of razor-sharp teeth. The Snalid queen sent out thousands of Snalid soldiers to bring back food for her colony. Don't let these things get near you, or you might become their next tasty snack!

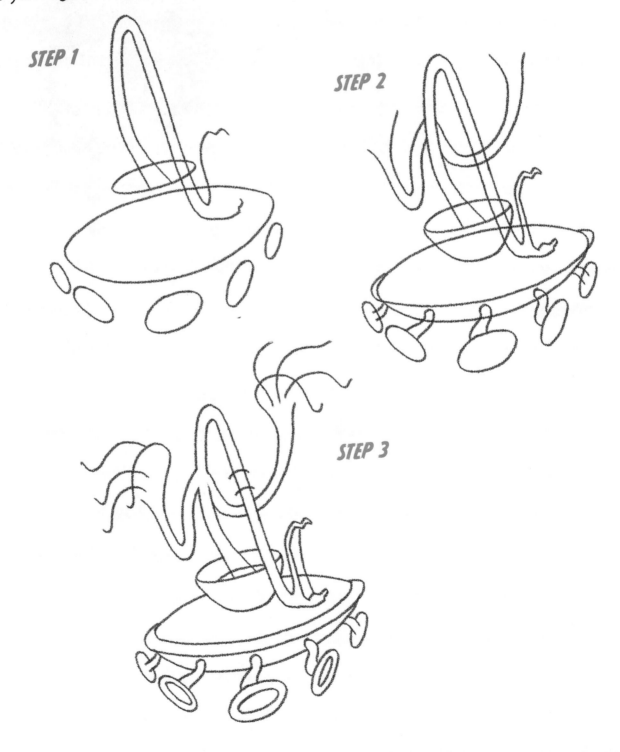

STEP 1

STEP 2

STEP 3

STEP 4

STEP 5

Once you've mastered this alien, draw a swarm of them getting ready to attack.

GORAXIANS

Goraxians are brutal warriors. They love to fight, and their micro-ray guns are deadly in battle. But if they lose radio contact with the Goraxian commander, they simply stop in place. If you're in a fight with a Goraxian, try to break off his antenna—it might be your only chance!

STEP 1

STEP 2

STEP 3

STEP 4

STEP 5

Try drawing the Goraxian commander! Give him some special armor or a radio communicator.

THE SIX-LEGGED SKREETCH

Few horrors are as terrifying as the Six-Legged Skreetch. Its name comes from the piercing shriek it uses to paralyze its prey. And its razor-sharp claws can rip through any armor. There's only one thing to do if you see one of these—RUN!

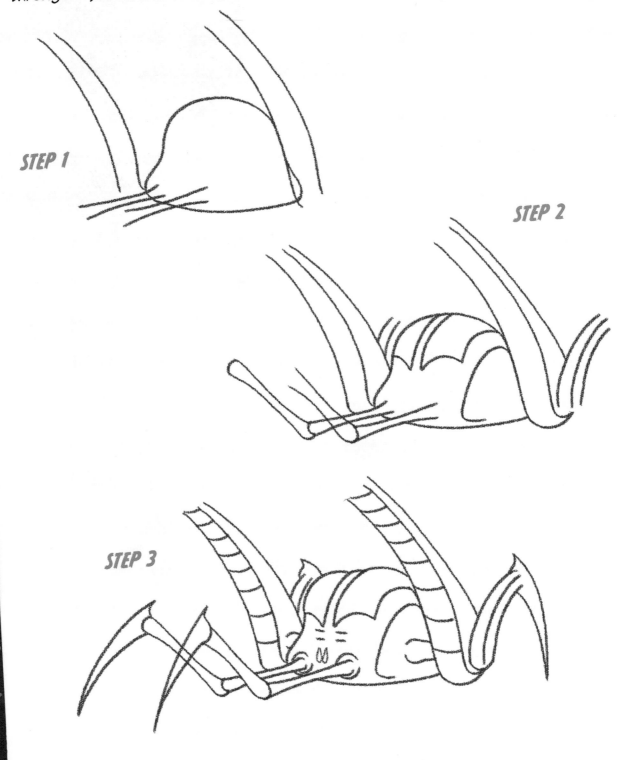

STEP 1

STEP 2

STEP 3

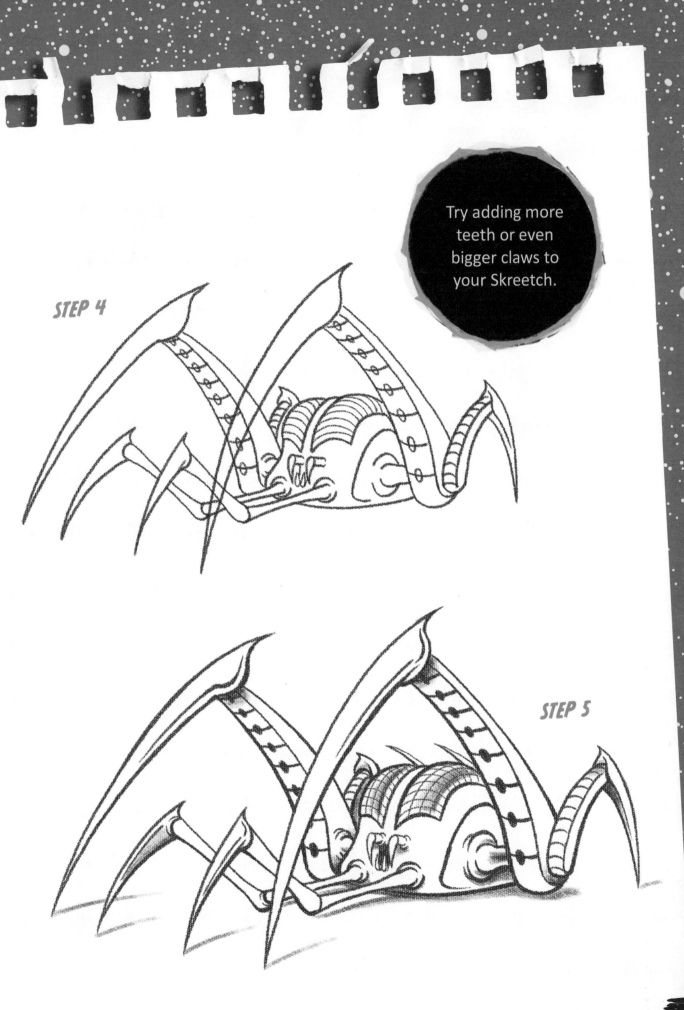

Try adding more teeth or even bigger claws to your Skreetch.

STEP 4

STEP 5

GRULDAN GLIDERS

The planet Gruldan is home to one of the galaxy's fiercest predators. The Gruldan Glider's dragonlike wings make it an excellent flyer. It hunts with heat-vision, and it kills its prey with venom sprayed from its tongue. You don't want to see one of these flying overhead!

STEP 1

STEP 2

STEP 3

STEP 4

STEP 5

Try showing a Gruldan Glider hunting down its next meal. What type of creature do you think it eats?

Qu24 Rocket

Got a large payload to haul? Then get yourself a Qu24 rocket! This rocket can lift more than 150,000 pounds (68 metric tons) of cargo into orbit. Used mostly by the kind-hearted Skrawk people, the rocket often carries food and supplies to nearby planets in need.

STEP 1

STEP 2

STEP 3

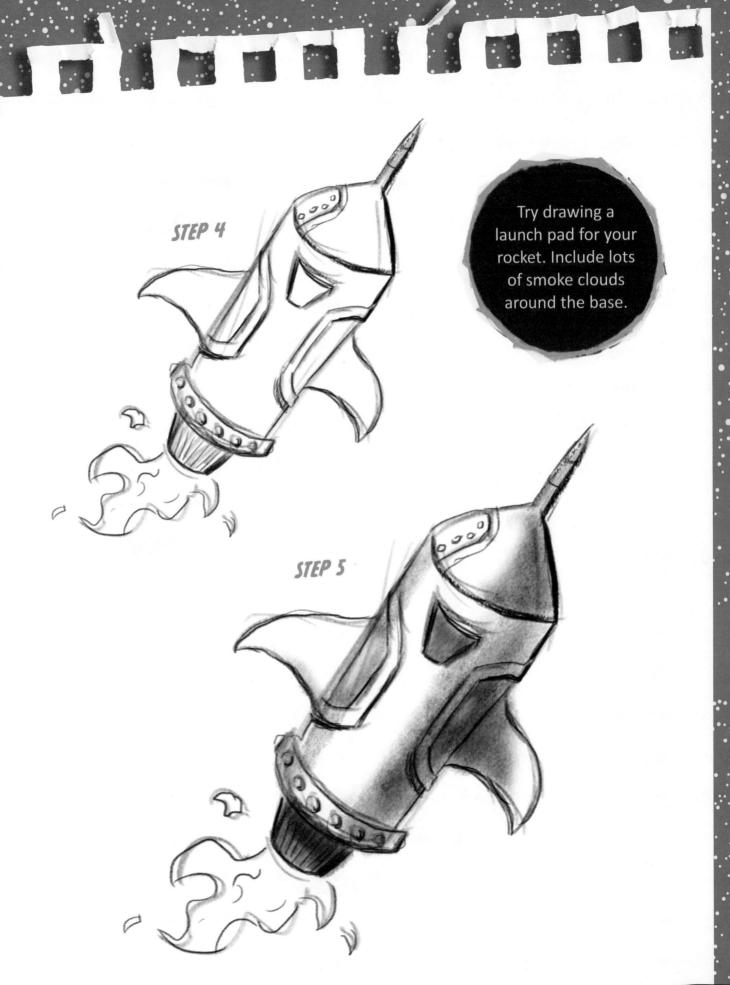

STEP 4

Try drawing a launch pad for your rocket. Include lots of smoke clouds around the base.

STEP 5

TENTACALLUS

Part frog, part octopus, and part who-knows-what. That's Tentacallus, a rarely seen underwater alien. Gentle-natured and shy, Tentacallus makes its home in the oceans of Planet Aquas. There it feasts on sea bugs and schools of tiny fish.

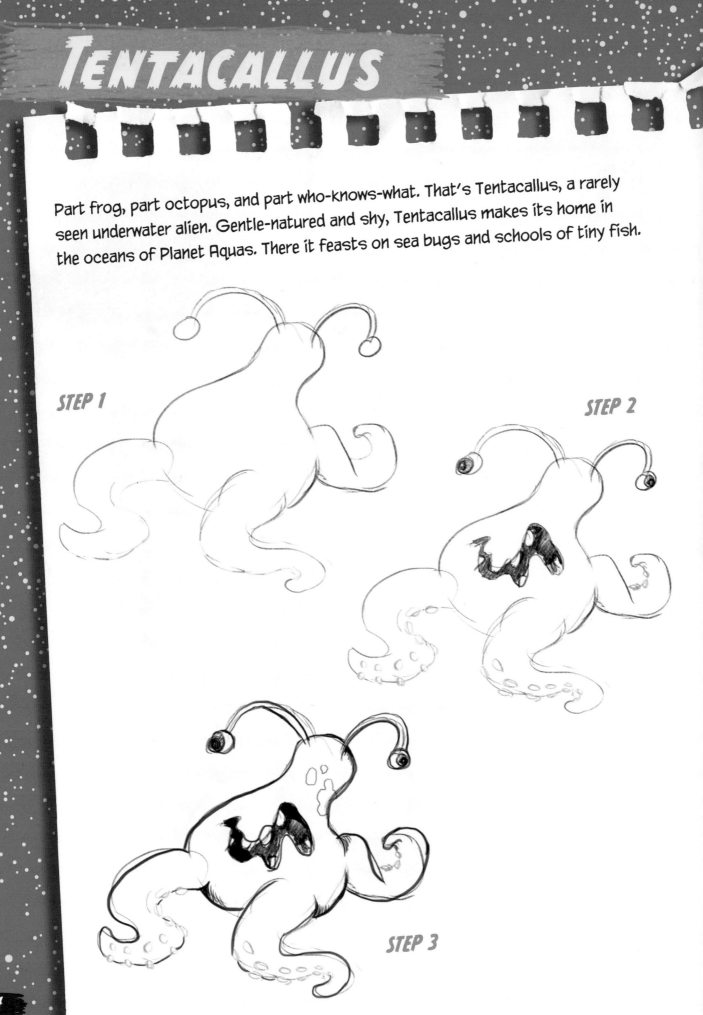

STEP 1

STEP 2

STEP 3

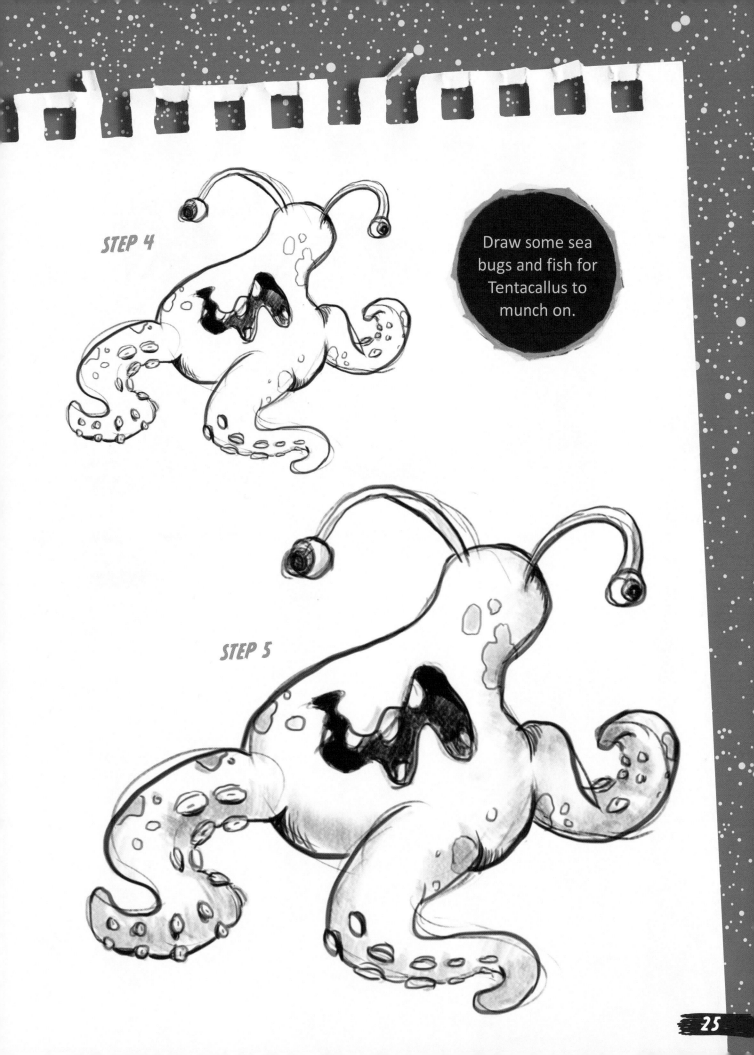

STEP 4

Draw some sea bugs and fish for Tentacallus to munch on.

STEP 5

UFO

Something zips around in the air. It hovers in place. It blinks. What is it? It's a UFO—an unidentified flying object. One of the most famous UFO sightings happened in 1947, in Roswell, New Mexico. A rancher found pieces of what he thought was an alien spaceship on his land.

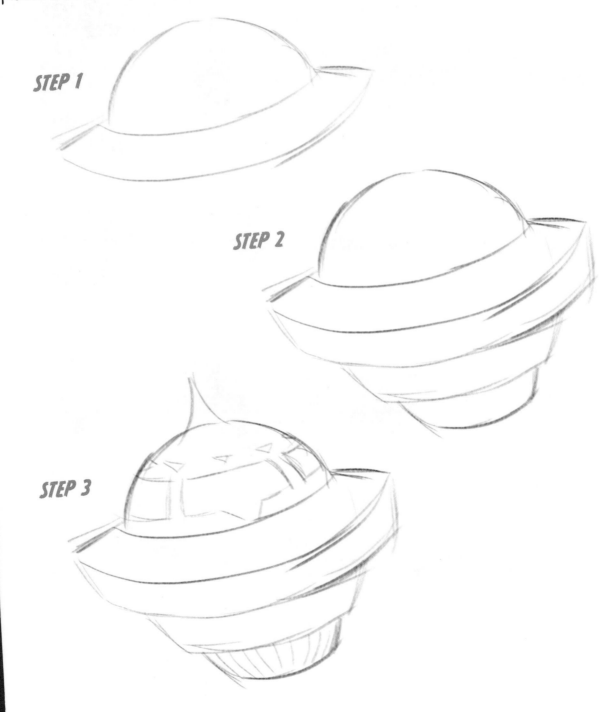

STEP 1

STEP 2

STEP 3

STEP 4

STEP 5

Once you've finished your UFO, draw the alien it belongs to. Is it friendly? Dangerous? Animal-like?

SPACE CAR

In some ways, aliens aren't much different than people. When they need to get somewhere fast, they hop in their car, just like we do. But the cool things about space cars? They fly. And they're powered by jet engines that move them faster than the speed of sound. ZOOM!

STEP 1

STEP 2

STEP 3

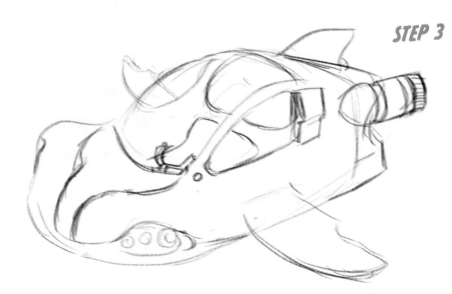

STEP 4

STEP 5

Draw your space car zipping around a bunch of planets and moons. Watch out for space rocks!

MADMIAN

The Madmians are tiny, tough aliens who live in the treetops of Planet Ooloc. What Madmians lack in size, they make up for in grit. They've got moves like monkeys and attack skills like great white sharks—with some weird alien stuff thrown in too.

STEP 1

STEP 2

STEP 3

STEP 4

STEP 5

Try drawing a community of Madmians swinging and leaping through an Oolocian forest.

CREATURE MOVER

On Earth, we call this a people mover. But in outer space, it's a creature mover. Like driverless shuttles or light-rail trains, creature movers take large groups of aliens from point A to point B. Some fly in any direction, like space cars. Others float above magnetic tracks.

STEP 1

STEP 2

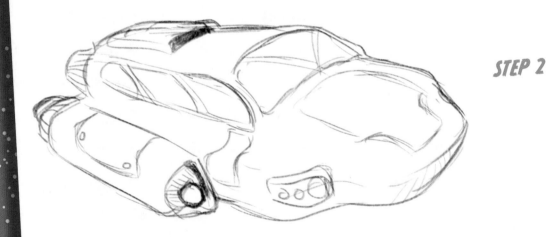

STEP 3

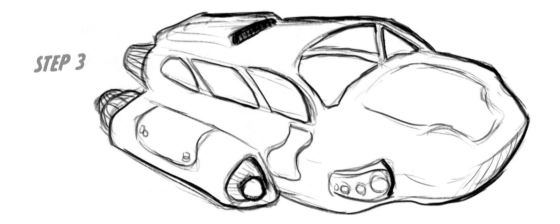

Once your creature mover is finished, draw a line of aliens, of all kinds, waiting to board.

STEP 4

STEP 5

XACTONON

A word of advice: Don't mess with a Xactonon (ZAK-toh-non)! With their razor-sharp claws and snapping jaws, Xactonons are one of the most feared aliens in any galaxy. They move fast and can leap straight up into the air. One blow from a Xactonon's fighting blade, and it's lights out!

STEP 1

Xactonons live in rocky, desert areas. Draw a home for your Xactonon (and don't forget the cacti!).

STEP 2

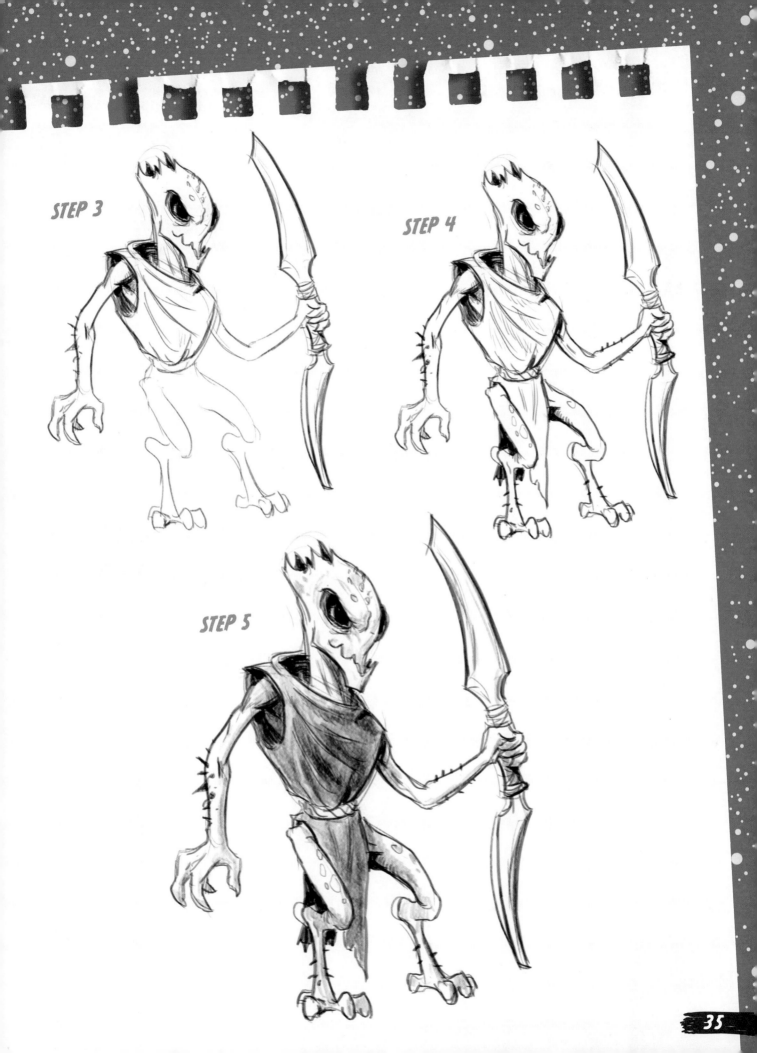

STEP 3

STEP 4

STEP 5

REPZID

No alien is cooler than a Repzid. Truth! From its goggle glasses to its long alligator tail, its trendy clothes to its jelly zapper (yep, it shoots strawberry jelly!). Repzids are fun-loving creatures and some of the most loyal alien friends you'll ever have.

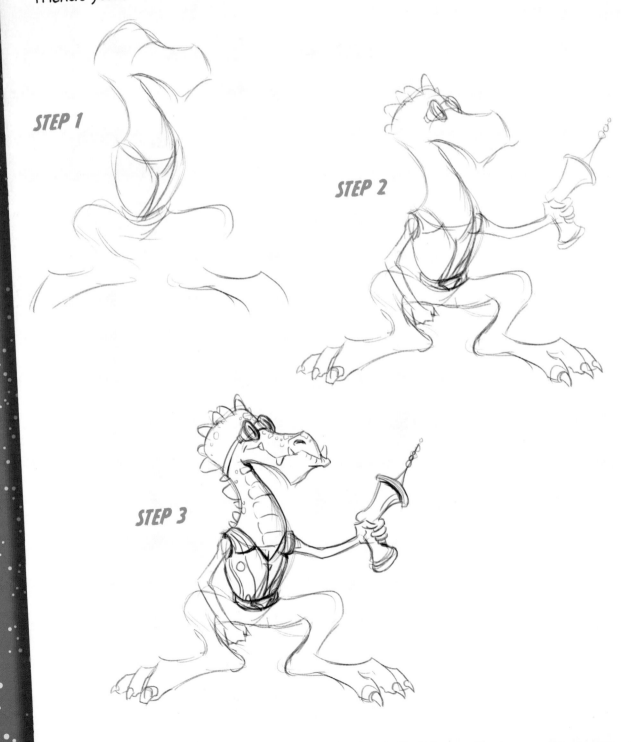

STEP 1

STEP 2

STEP 3

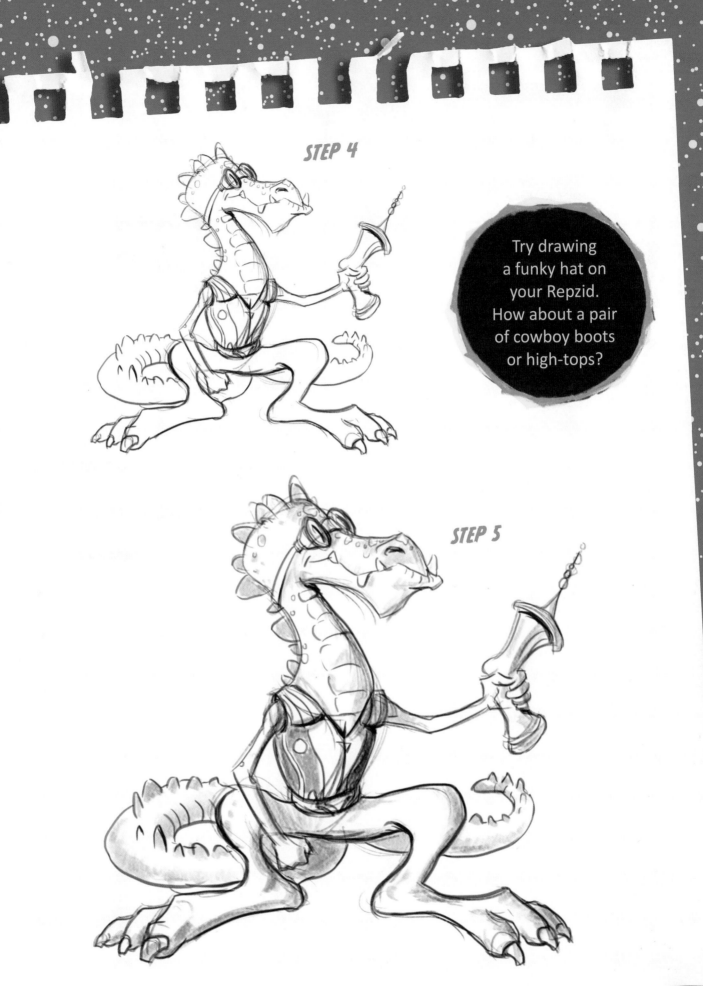

STEP 4

Try drawing a funky hat on your Repzid. How about a pair of cowboy boots or high-tops?

STEP 5

SPACE STATION

Madmians use this space station to study plant growth in space. Decades of hot, dry weather on the Madmians' home planet, Ooloc, have nearly wiped out the food supply. The work being done in the space station is key to the Madmians' survival.

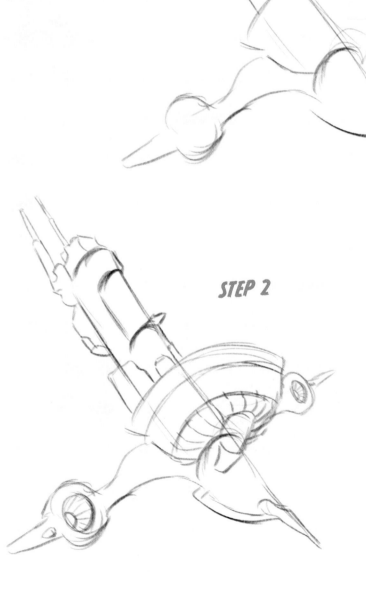

STEP 1

STEP 2

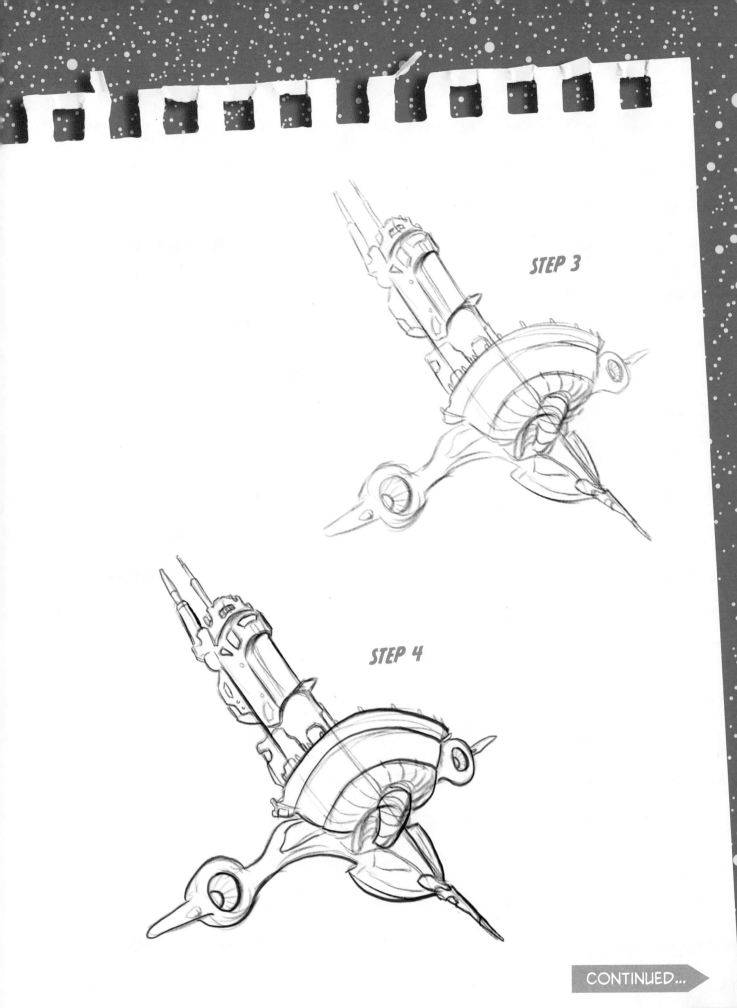

STEP 3

STEP 4

CONTINUED...

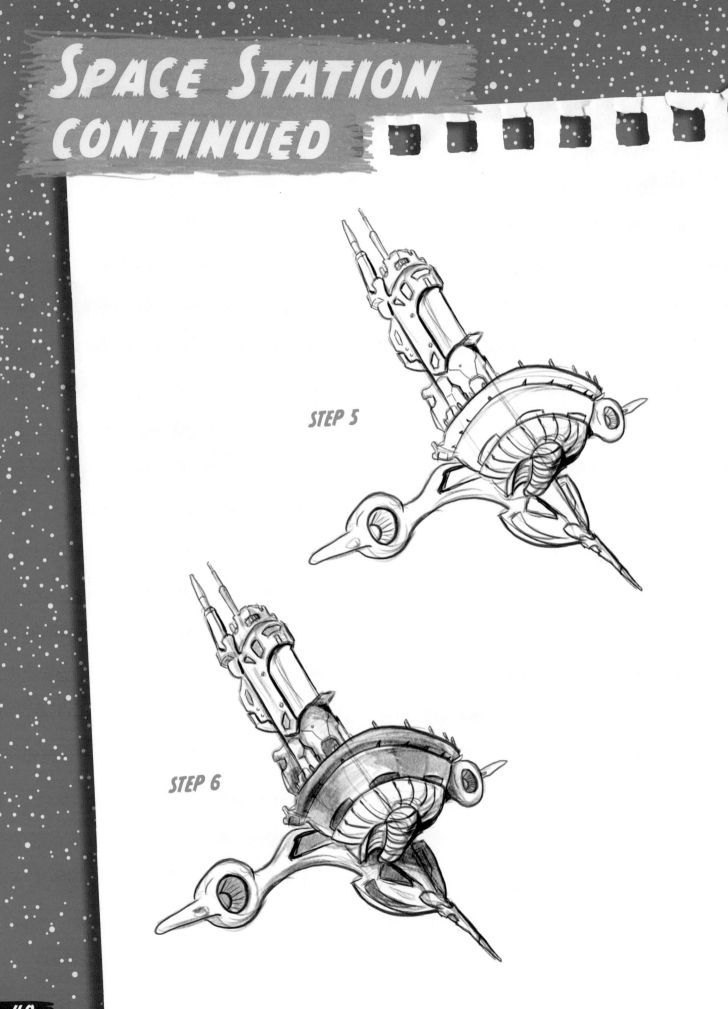

STEP 5

STEP 6

After you've drawn the space station from the outside, sketch the view from the inside.

STEP 7

SHAHLAHZ, THE BIONIC GIRL

Long ago, a bad accident severely injured a Florida girl named Shayla Glueck. Doctors rebuilt much of her body with mechanical parts and trained her to fight crime. With her super-strong arms, lightning-fast legs, and X-ray vision, Shayla is now known as Shahlahz, the Bionic Girl.

STEP 1

STEP 2

STEP 3

STEP 4

CONTINUED...

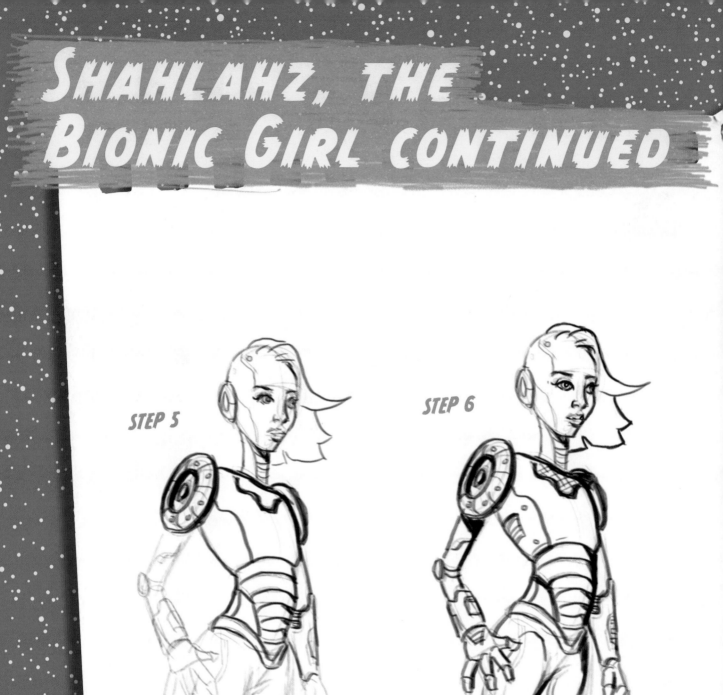

STEP 5

STEP 6

STEP 7

Show off Shahlahz's strength by drawing her smashing through a wall or lifting a bus over her head.

AMAZING ROBOTS

THERE ARE GOOD ROBOTS AND BAD ROBOTS. Helpful and not-so-helpful. The 10 amazing robots in this section represent both kinds. Some fight crime, clean homes, and warn people of danger. Others break the law, destroy homes (and whole planets!), and crush any people who get in their way.

After you've learned to draw these robots, freestyle your own. **USE YOUR IMAGINATION** and see what sorts of awesome robots you can create. Are they helpful or destructive? What do they do? Where do they live? What are their names? What makes them special?

THE BOB-v2.5

Danger! Danger! The BOB-v2.5 isn't fast. And he doesn't carry any weapons. But he's very loyal and always warns you when trouble is near. After all, once a best friend, always a best friend!

STEP 1

STEP 2

STEP 3

STEP 4

This BOB-v2.5 won't get very far without legs! Draw a sturdy pair, with wheels for feet.

STEP 5

MECH-TROOPERS

Mech-Troopers were designed to keep the streets safe from crime. But they soon began keeping the peace by forcing people to stay in their homes. Now everyone hopes the central command unit will be destroyed so people can live their lives in freedom again.

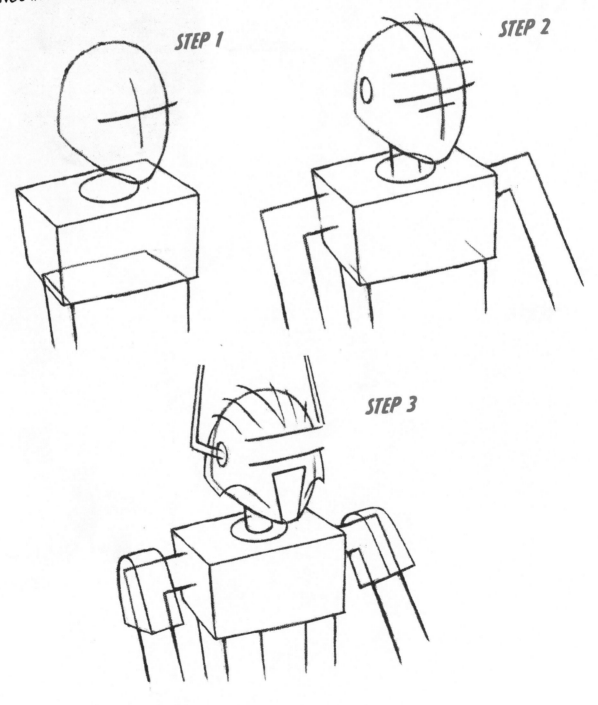

STEP 1

STEP 2

STEP 3

STEP 4

After drawing this robot, try drawing a bunch of them patrolling a city street.

STEP 5

THE FXR-UPR

Don't have time for pesky chores? Get yourself the new FXR-UPR! This little robot can do any job with its wide variety of arm attachments. But be sure to keep an eye on it. The FXR-UPR has been known to reprogram itself and destroy its owner's home.

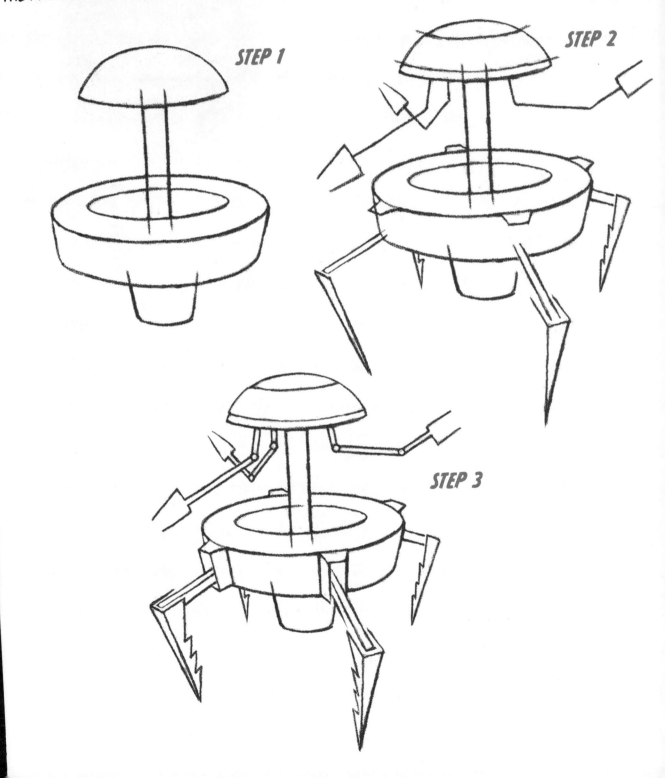

STEP 1

STEP 2

STEP 3

STEP 4

Add some tools to the FXR-UPR's arms, like a shovel or saw. Maybe a broom, drill, or vacuum!

STEP 5

THE ECHO-4000

No secret is safe with the ECHO-4000 around. It may look harmless, but it can easily capture and decode your most secret messages. Be careful what you say when one of these is nearby!

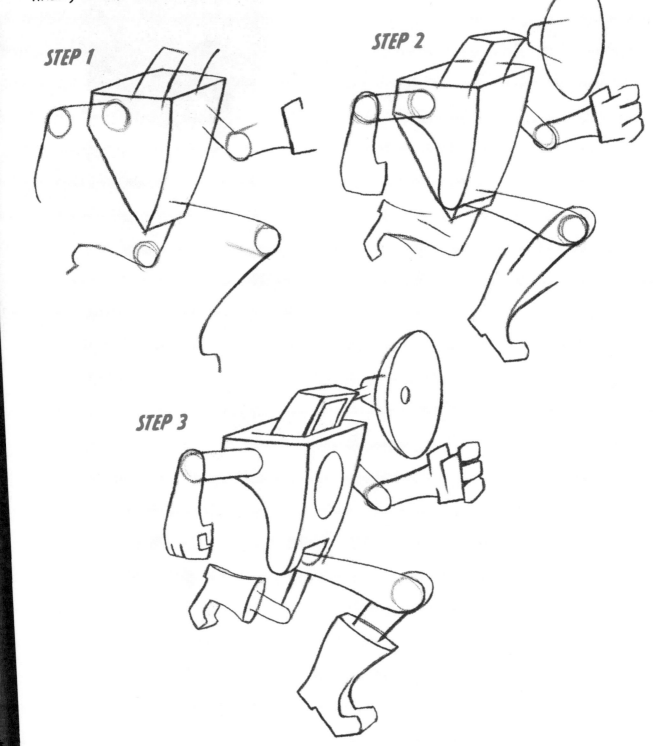

STEP 1

STEP 2

STEP 3

When you've learned to draw this robot, add some even bigger, crazier antennae.

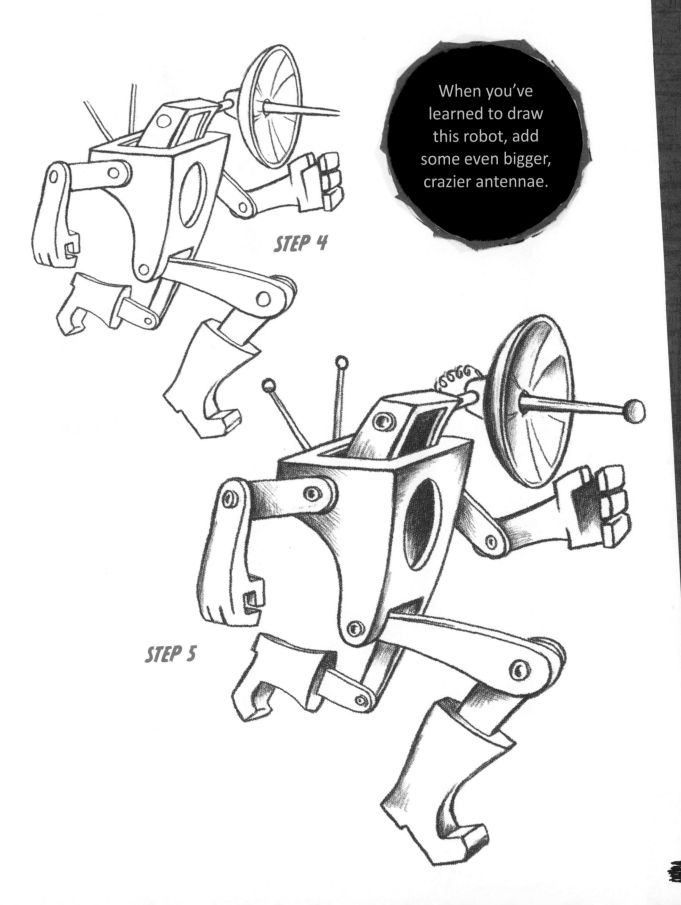

STEP 4

STEP 5

THE TENTACLE TERROR X-22

The Tentacle Terror X-22 is slippery and quick. Its twisting, snakelike arms are lightning fast. Be careful! It can snatch you up and carry you off before you know what's happening!

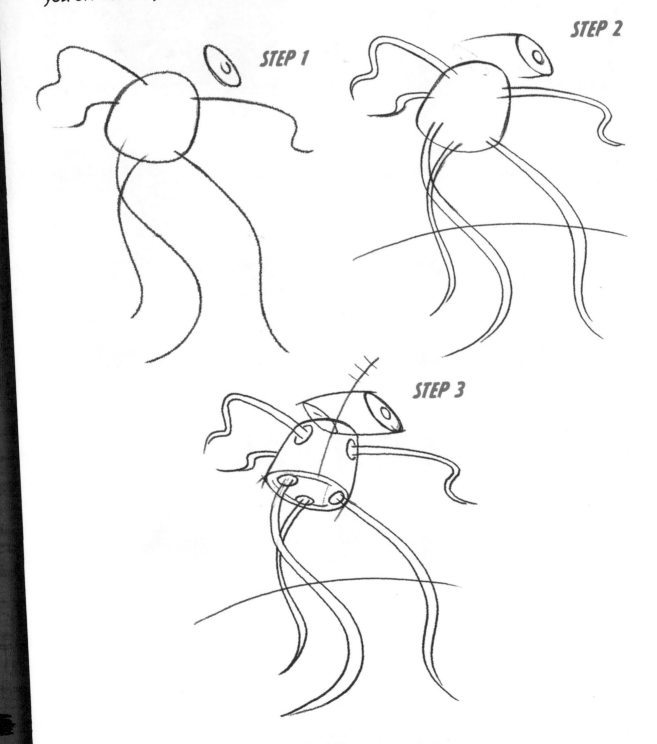

STEP 1

STEP 2

STEP 3

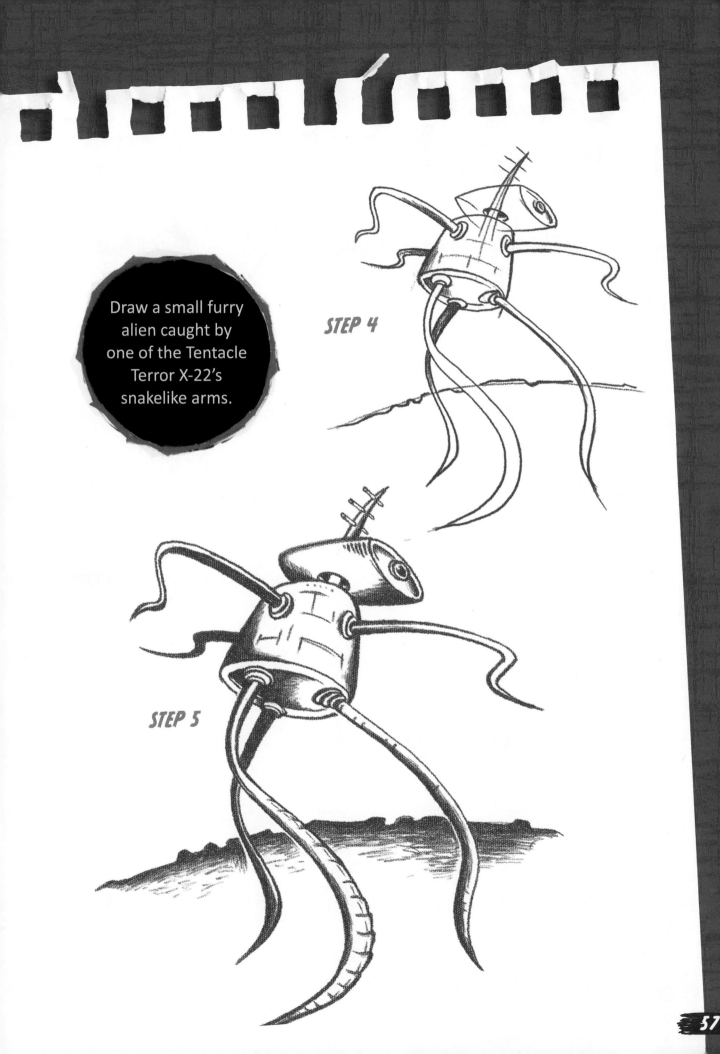

Draw a small furry alien caught by one of the Tentacle Terror X-22's snakelike arms.

STEP 4

STEP 5

BIO-SCOUT MK5

The planet Thorgo is a barren place. There is little food or water there. The Thorgons created the Bio-Scout MK5 model to search the galaxy and gather new resources. These mechanical menaces have stripped many worlds of all life. Find a good place to hide if you see one of these!

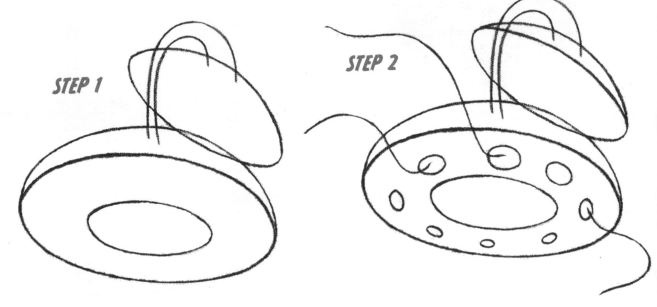

STEP 1

STEP 2

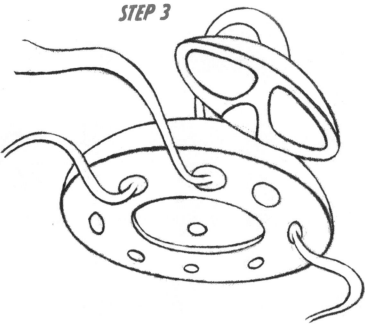

STEP 3

STEP 4

STEP 5

Try drawing this robot as it stuffs its cargo bay with all sorts of plants and animals.

PACIFIER P-17s

In the year 2432, civil war rocks the planet Venus. Pacifier P-17s were created to bring peace. But the machines don't know friend from foe. They crush anyone in their way with their giant mechanical claws.

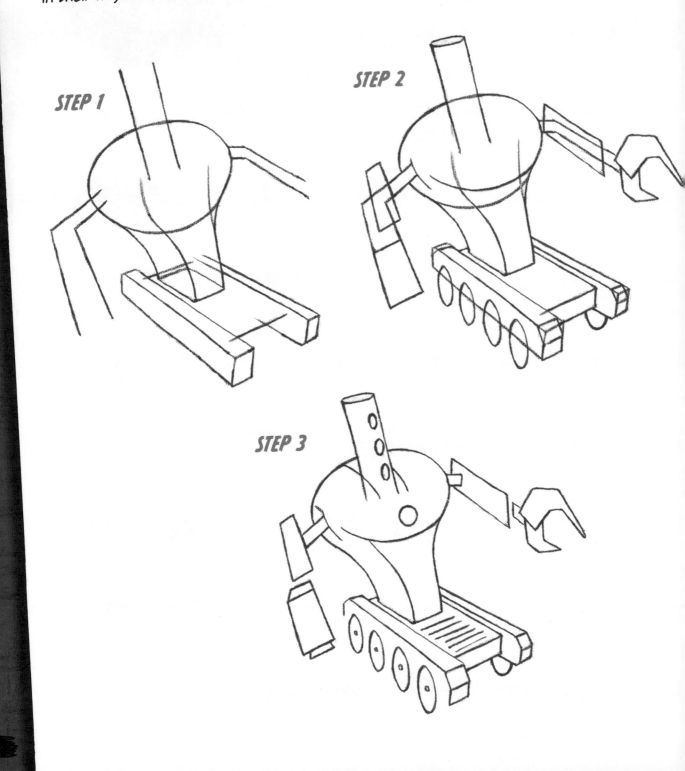

STEP 1

STEP 2

STEP 3

STEP 4

STEP 5

Try drawing the Pacifier P-17 crushing one of the other robots in this section.

THE JET DEFENDER-7T

Look! Is that a rocket? No, it's the new Jet Defender-7t! It can travel thousands of miles in just seconds with its rocket-powered feet. Don't break the law, or you might be the next one it throws in prison.

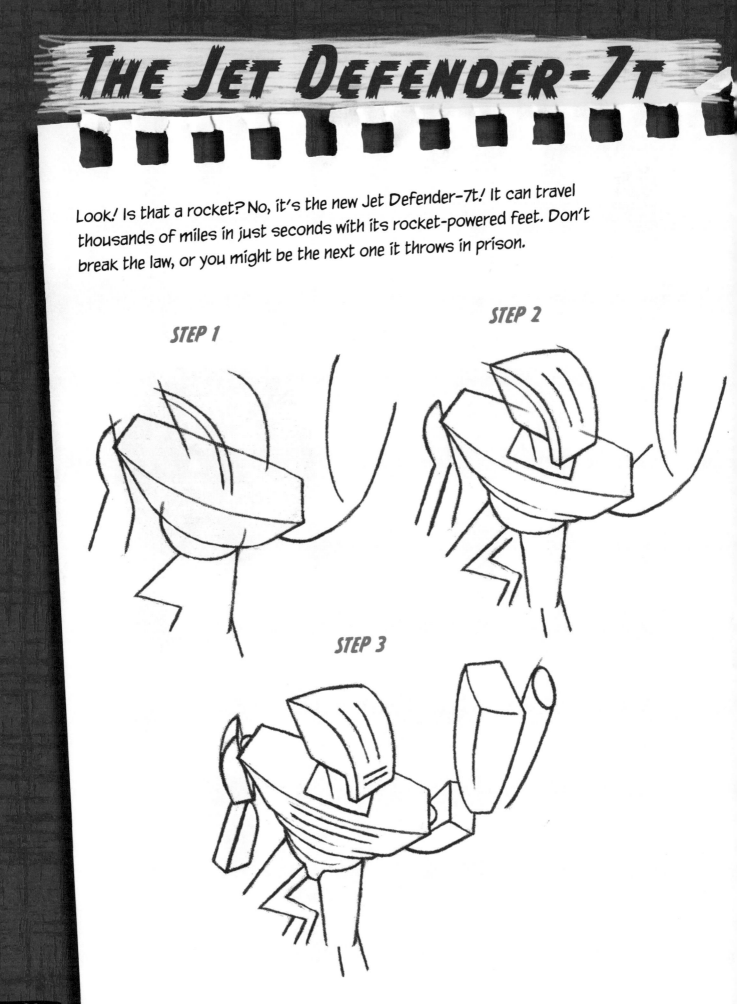

STEP 1

STEP 2

STEP 3

STEP 4

Two are better than one! Help your robot keep the peace by drawing a partner for it.

STEP 5

RAMPAGE-XT3

Rampage-XT3 has been seen in many cities in Asia. This giant robot can take the shape of a bulldozer, a tank, or even a jet plane. It can show up anywhere, at any time. But it's easy to follow, due to the path of destruction it always leaves behind.

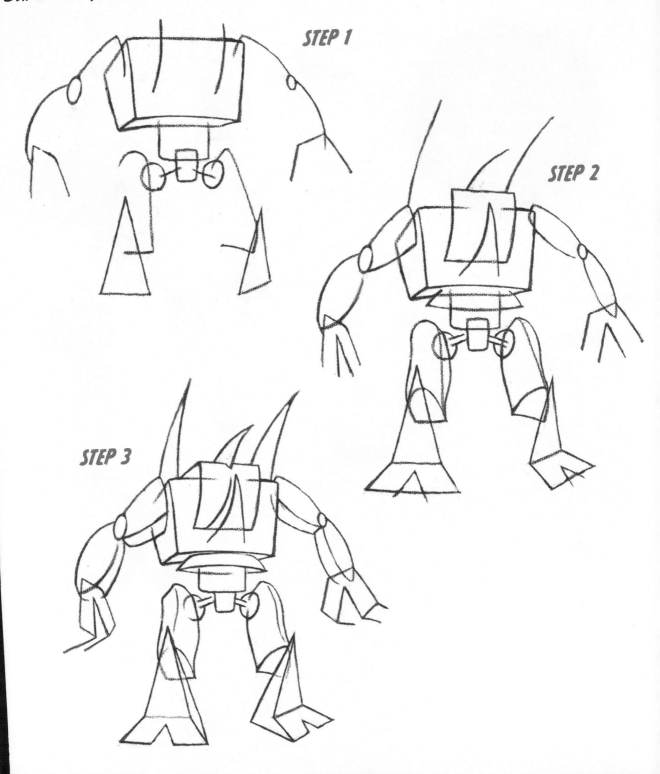

STEP 1

STEP 2

STEP 3

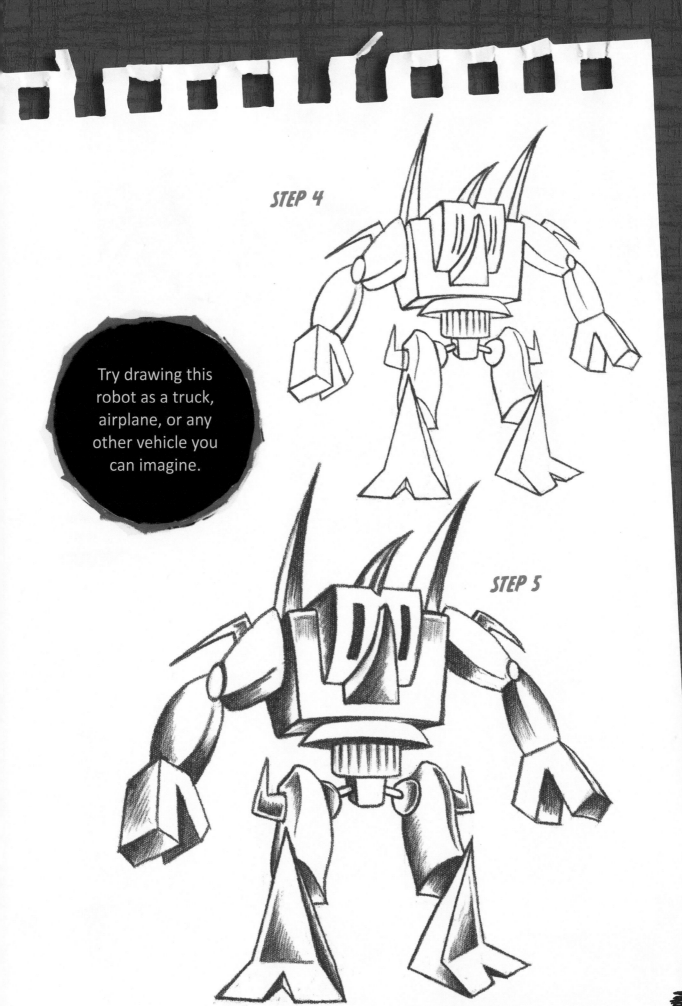

STEP 4

Try drawing this robot as a truck, airplane, or any other vehicle you can imagine.

STEP 5

THE BUZZ-BOT 6

The giant Buzz-Bot 6 from the planet Praxis-2 has many weapons to use. Deadly spikes cover its arms for defense. And its huge, razor-sharp pincers can easily rip through the thickest armor. Don't make this thing angry, or you'll be sorry!

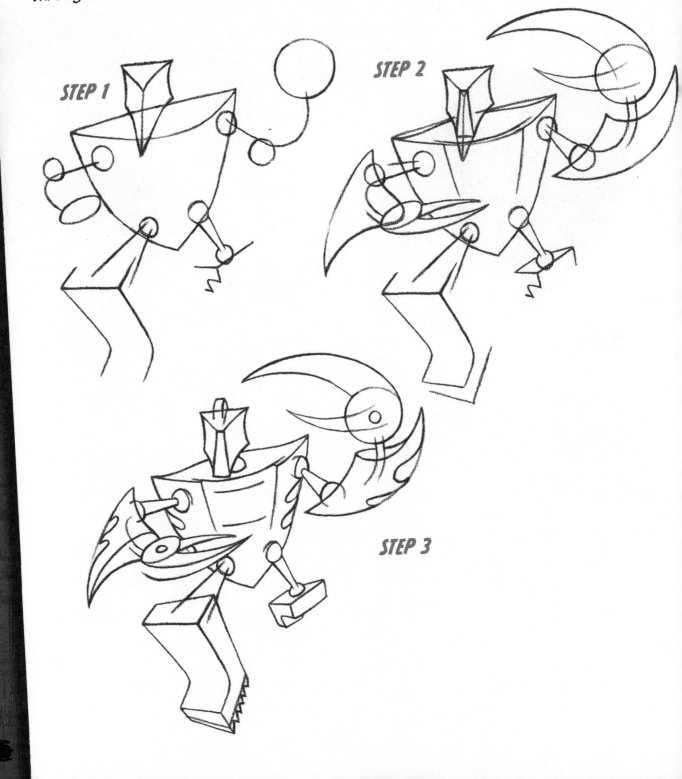

STEP 1

STEP 2

STEP 3

STEP 4

Draw a battle between this giant and the Tentacle Terror X-22 from pages 56–57.

STEP 5

MANGA WARRIORS

WHEN YOU HEAR THE TERM "COMIC BOOK," WHAT'S THE FIRST THING YOU THINK OF? Superheroes like Spiderman and Black Panther? Wonder Woman and Batman? How about the Archie, Babymouse, or Bone series? There are many kinds of comics, but one of the most popular is called manga.

Manga are Japanese comics that have a very special style. Even though manga first started in Japan, they're read all around the world today. Manga can be about almost anything, but warriors are common characters, like the **BRAVE, FIERCE FIGHTERS** in this section.

JAD

Faces are important when drawing manga. Large eyes, small noses, and pointed chins are common in most manga characters. Facial expressions show how a character feels. Here you can see that Jad isn't happy.

STEP 1

STEP 2

STEP 3

When you're done with Jad's face, draw the rest of his body.

STEP 4

STEP 5

SARYNA

Saryna's eyes are larger than Jad's. They show even more emotion. Her face is rounder, and her nose is smaller too. Her frowning eyebrows and unhappy mouth show she's upset about something.

STEP 1

STEP 2

STEP 3

After practicing this drawing, give Saryna some different hairstyles or facial expressions.

STEP 4

STEP 5

KARATE PRACTICE

Like most warriors, Jad practices his martial arts skills daily. His powerful arms and swift karate moves can defend almost any attack. He wants to have the fastest hands in the land.

STEP 1

STEP 2

STEP 3

STEP 4

Draw the rest of Jad's body and show him practicing some karate punches.

STEP 5

SWORD PRACTICE

Saryna hopes to one day be a mighty hero like her father. She has chosen a katana sword to help defend her village. She isn't as strong or fast as Jad, but she is deadly with a weapon in her hands.

STEP 1

STEP 2

STEP 3

What other poses could Saryna strike with her sword? Draw them!

STEP 4

STEP 5

HIROTO

Through many years of practice and lots of hard work, Hiroto became a martial arts master. When faced with danger, he can defeat enemies in the blink of an eye. His fierceness and speed are legendary in his homeland.

STEP 1

STEP 2

STEP 3

Show off Hiroto's skills by giving him some ninjas to fight against.

STEP 4

STEP 5

LINWEYA

Linweya has worked hard to become a master of the sword. She is a deadly foe with any blade. Luckily, she uses her talents only to defend the innocent. As with Hiroto, the people of her homeland are awed by her heroic deeds.

STEP 1

STEP 2

STEP 3

Draw Linweya protecting a small family from an army of evil warriors.

STEP 4

STEP 5

MARAGI

Maragi is old—very old. Legends say he was once an evil wizard. As punishment, he was cursed to live forever. Now he teaches his students the honorable ways of the warrior code. He hopes to one day be released from his curse and finally be at rest.

STEP 1

STEP 2

STEP 3

After practicing this drawing, show Maragi teaching new moves to a young warrior.

STEP 4

STEP 5

YUNA

Yuna is one of Maragi's best students. She is strong-willed, and often disobeys her parents. But with Maragi's teaching, Yuna is quickly becoming a highly skilled fighter. She is especially talented with her favorite weapon—the nunchaku.

STEP 1

STEP 2

STEP 3

Try giving Yuna some new, fierce moves to use with her nunchaku.

STEP 4

STEP 5

GENERAL KUROK

The ways of the warrior will continue in the future. In the year 2235, General Kurok commands the battleship *Blazing Arkon*. Through studying history's greatest warriors, he has become the mightiest commander to ever travel the stars.

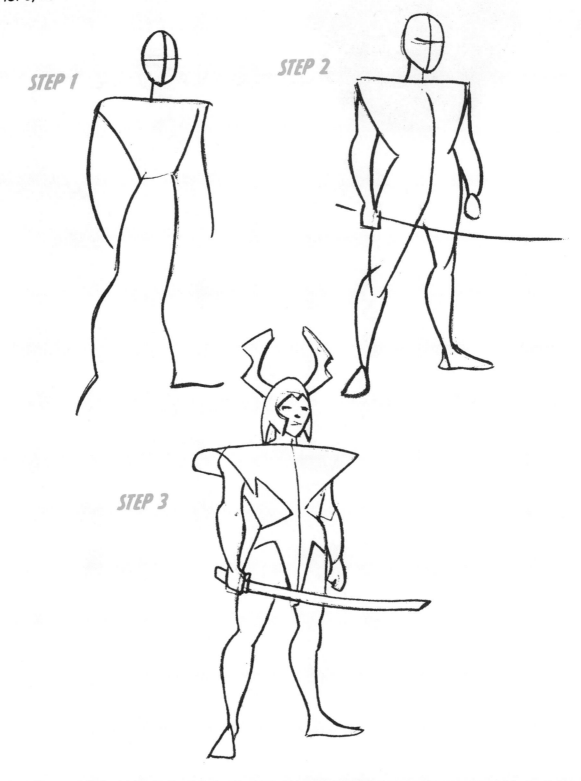

STEP 1

STEP 2

STEP 3

Design your own armor for General Kurok to wear. Try adding spikes, horns, or claws.

STEP 4

STEP 5

GHINSHU

Ghinshu is a master of the blade. He has fought in many battles in many lands. His body bears many scars, and he recently lost an eye battling a skilled foe. But in spite of his reduced vision, Ghinshu remains a deadly fighter with his swords.

STEP 1

STEP 2

STEP 3

STEP 4

Try drawing Ghinshu and his swords in an epic duel with another warrior.

STEP 5

EPIC BATTLES

The Warriors of the Crescent Moon long fought against all injustice and evil. But one day the Black Emperor sent his emissary to dispose of those who stood against him. The epic battles between the warriors and the Black Emissary later became the stuff of legend.

STEP 1

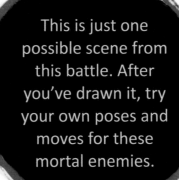

This is just one possible scene from this battle. After you've drawn it, try your own poses and moves for these mortal enemies.

STEP 2

STEP 3

CONTINUED...

EPIC BATTLES CONTINUED

STEP 4

STEP 5

STEP 6

STEP 7

VEHICLES

DO YOU HAVE SOMEWHERE TO GO BUT DON'T KNOW HOW TO GET THERE? How about hopping onto a helicopter? Cruising on a ship? Burning rubber in a muscle car or crushing traffic in a monster truck? The 10 vehicles in this section are fueled up and ready for you (and your pencil). Pick your favorite!

On land, through the air, and across and beneath the sea . . . That's where these drawing projects will take you. Grab some fresh paper, buckle up, and

ENJOY THE RIDE!

The specs for this ballistic missile submarine sound made up, But they're not! The sub is almost two football fields long and as wide as a three-lane highway. It can sail deeper than 800 feet (244 meters). It carries about 150 sailors for months at a time. And it makes oxygen for the crew too.

STEP 1

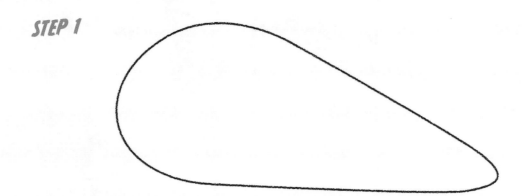

STEP 2

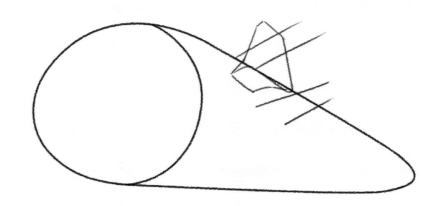

STEP 3

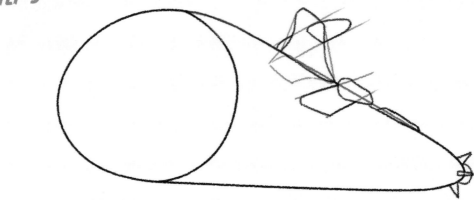

STEP 4

With what sorts of creatures does your sub share the sea? Whales? Giant jellyfish? Great white sharks? Draw them!

STEP 5

FIGHTER JET

By the time you hear this jet, it's gone! Jet speeds are often measured in Mach numbers. Mach 1 is equal to the speed of sound in air. How fast is that? When the air temperature is 70 degrees Fahrenheit (21 degrees Celsius), the speed of sound is about 770 miles (1,239 kilometers) per hour!

STEP 1

STEP 2

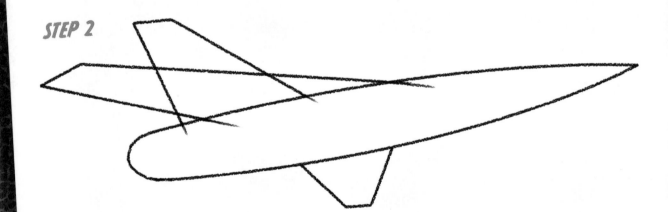

STEP 3

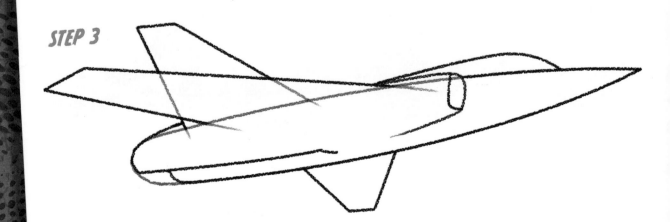

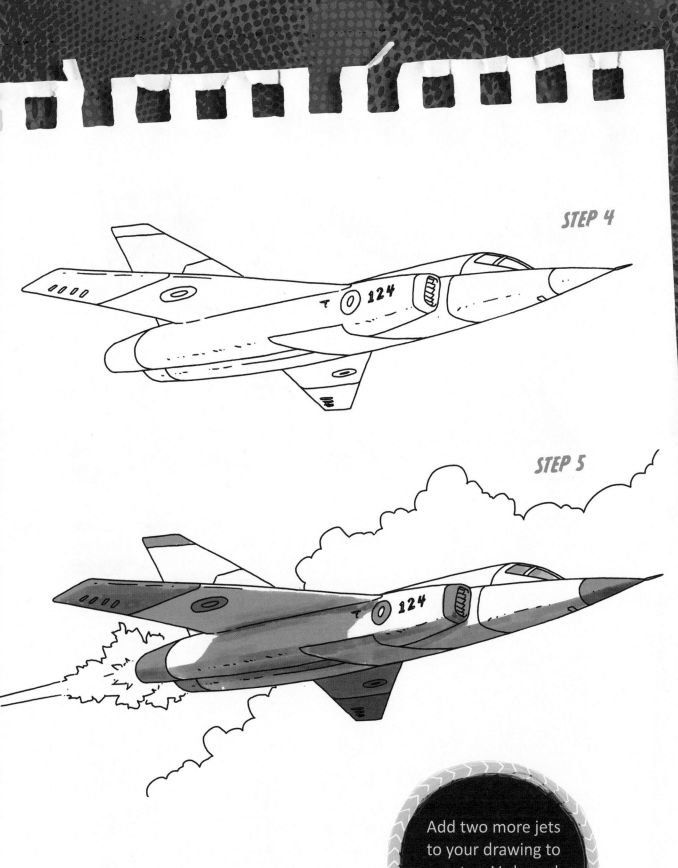

STEP 4

STEP 5

Add two more jets to your drawing to create a V-shaped formation (pattern) called a Vic.

CRUISE SHIP

Unlike *Titanic*, which sank in the Atlantic Ocean in 1912, *this* cruise ship sails safely past the icebergs. Today's cruise ships are like cities on the water. They have restaurants, shops, movie theaters, pools, fitness centers, and more. The largest ships can carry nearly 7,000 passengers!

STEP 1

STEP 2
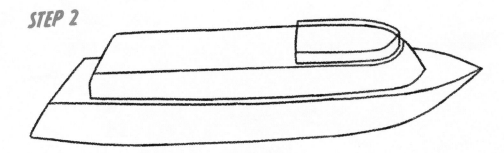

STEP 3
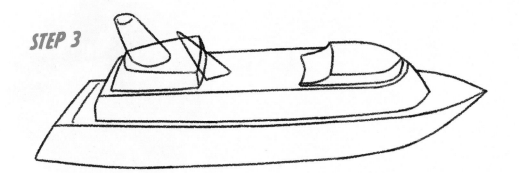

STEP 4

Draw your
ship pulling into
a port (a town
or city along
the water).

STEP 5

BIPLANE

The biplane is named for its two sets of fixed wings—*bi* meaning "two."
It's probably best known for its use during World War I (1914-1918).
A type of British biplane called the Sopwith Camel was especially famous.
No airplane shot down more German aircraft than it did.

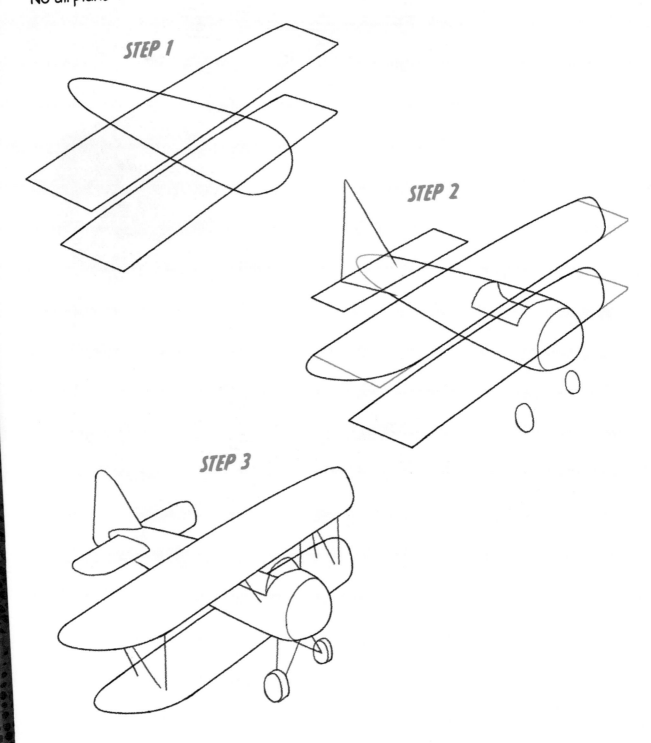

STEP 1

STEP 2

STEP 3

STEP 4

Today, biplanes are often used for air-show stunts (aerobatics). Try drawing your plane doing a smoky loop or corkscrew.

STEP 5

MONSTER TRUCK

If you like big, nasty-looking vehicles, look no further. With an ear-busting roar and ridiculously huge tires, this monster truck crushes anything in its path. Average monster truck tires measure 66 inches (168 centimeters) tall. But a truck called Bigfoot 5 set a world record. Its beastly rubber donuts measured 120 INCHES (305 CM) tall!

STEP 1

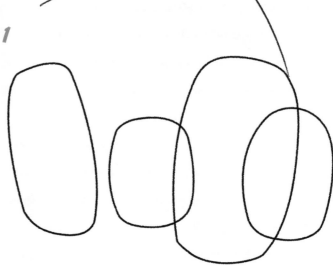

STEP 2

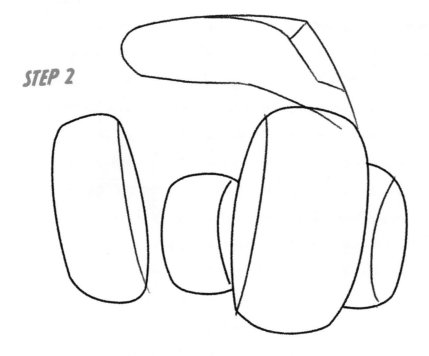

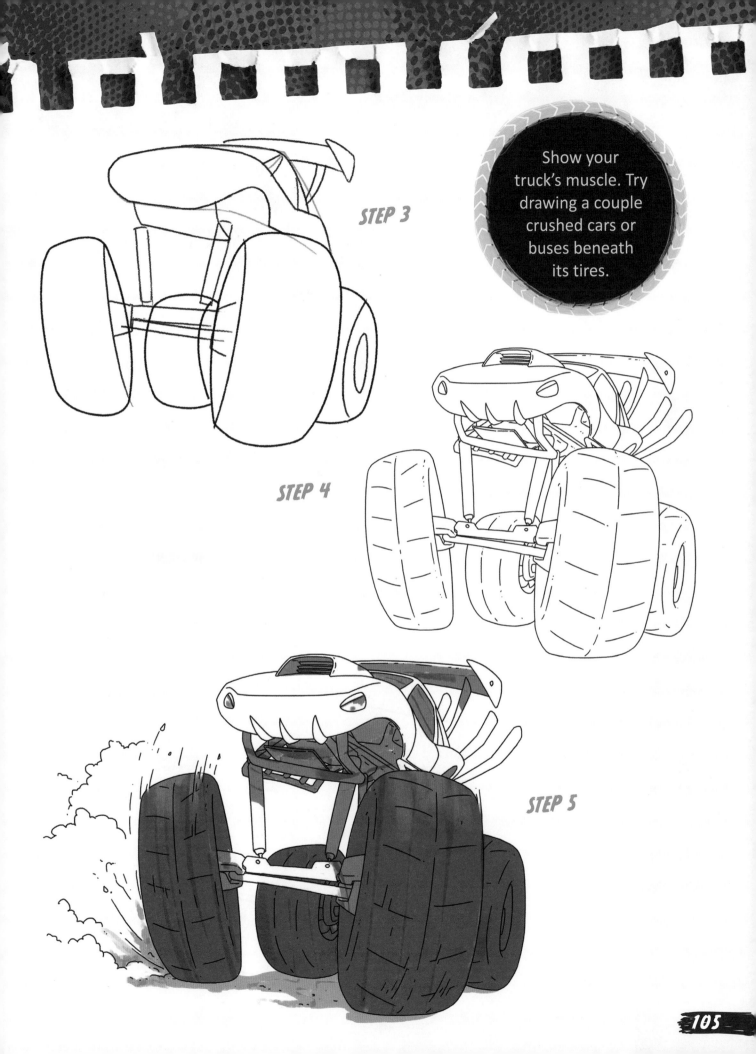

STEP 3

Show your truck's muscle. Try drawing a couple crushed cars or buses beneath its tires.

STEP 4

STEP 5

HELICOPTER

Have to get to a hard-to-reach place, fast? Call in a helicopter! From rescues in the mountains to rescues at sea, helicopters have a long history of saving the day. Why? They need little space (or time) for taking off and landing. They can hover in place. And they move fast over distances.

STEP 1

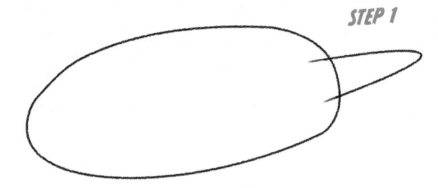

STEP 2

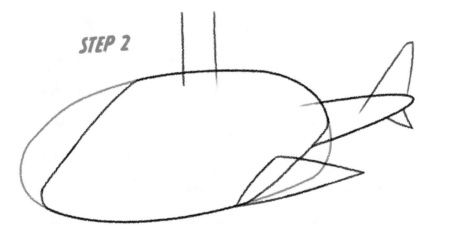

STEP 3

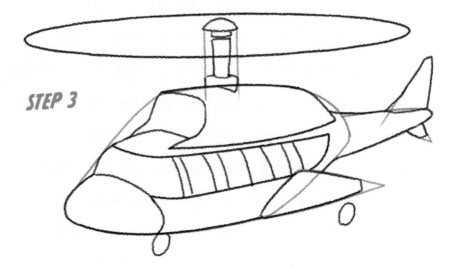

STEP 4

Draw a rescue scene for your helicopter. Is it in a big city? A canyon? A tropical island?

STEP 5

TALL SHIP

Before ships had engines powered by steam or gas, they used the wind. Sailors attached, or rigged, fabric sails to poles called masts. Pirates loved ships like this two-masted, square-rigged beauty. Called a brig, the ship moved quickly—perfect for attacking and looting other ships.

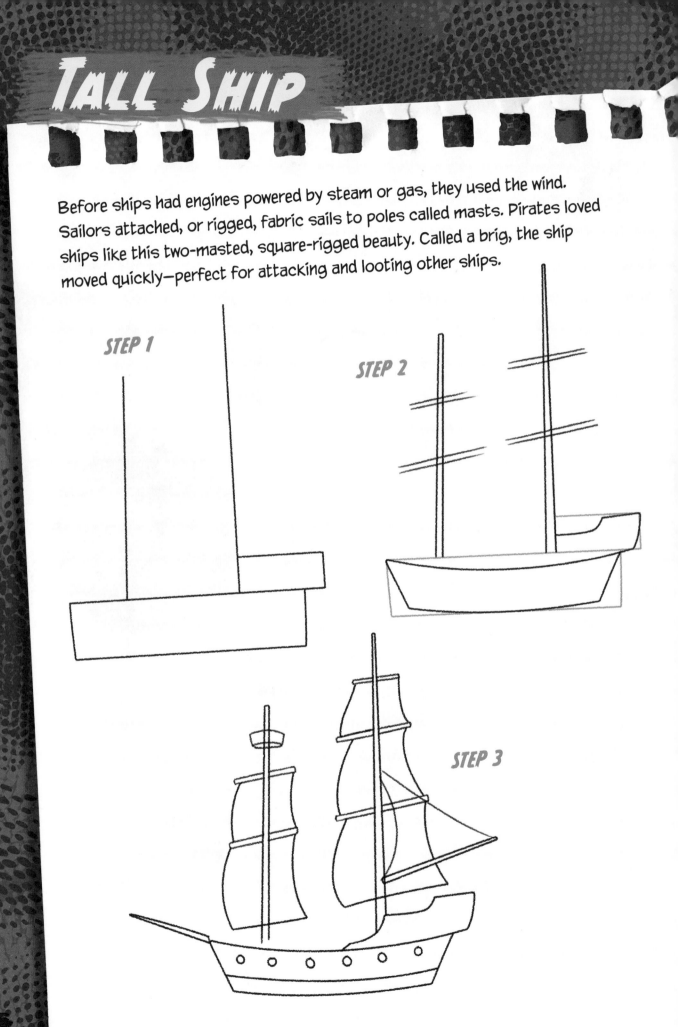

STEP 1

STEP 2

STEP 3

What lies in
the waters beneath
your ship? Draw a
giant octopus or your
own imaginary
sea monster.

STEP 4

STEP 5

MUSCLE CAR

Hear that growl? That deep rumble? A muscle car is coming! Muscle cars get their name from their powerful, high-performance engines. They first hit the streets in the 1960s and 1970s. Some of the meanest machines included the Pontiac GTO, the Chevy Camaro, and the Shelby Mustang.

STEP 1

STEP 2

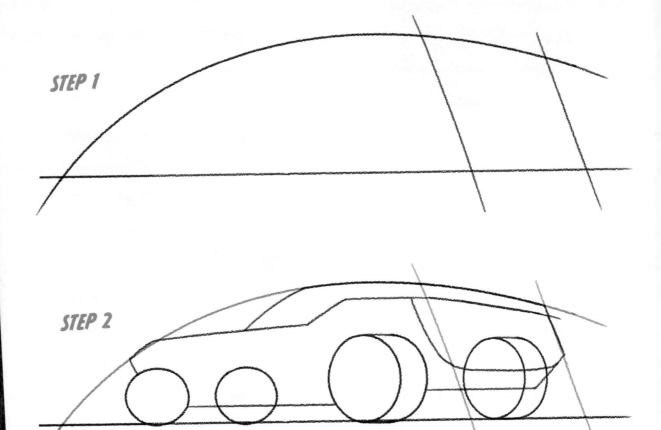

STEP 3

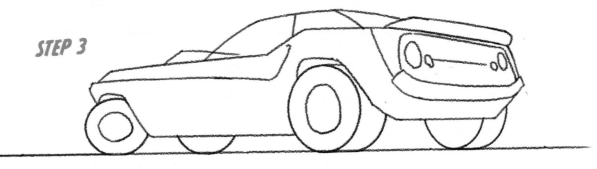

STEP 4

After you've finished drawing your car, give it a custom paint job. Add stripes, flames, or lightning bolts.

STEP 5

MOTORCYCLE

One of the coolest kinds of motorcycles is the leaning three-wheeler. It's also called a reverse trike. With two wheels in front and one in back, this bike loves to hug the road. It leans into curves just like a two-wheel motorcycle, but with better balance. And its rocket-like power leaves other bikes in the dust.

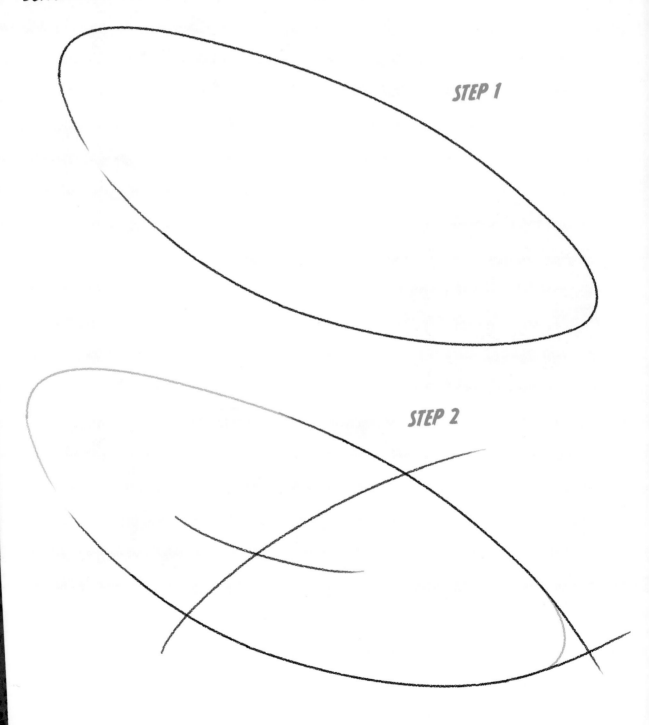

STEP 1

STEP 2

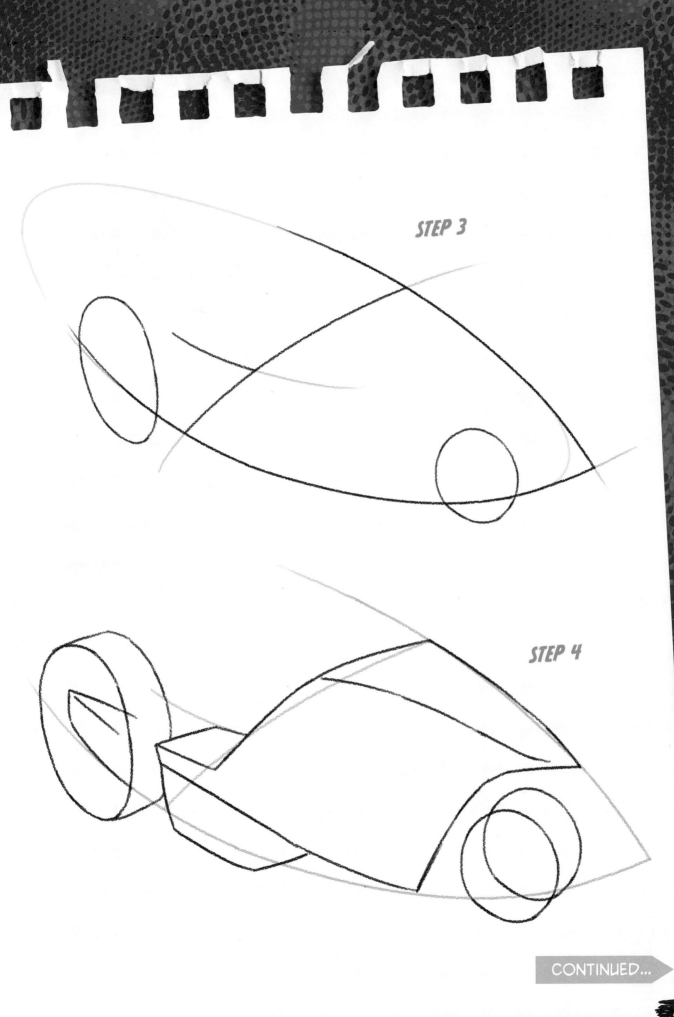

STEP 3

STEP 4

CONTINUED...

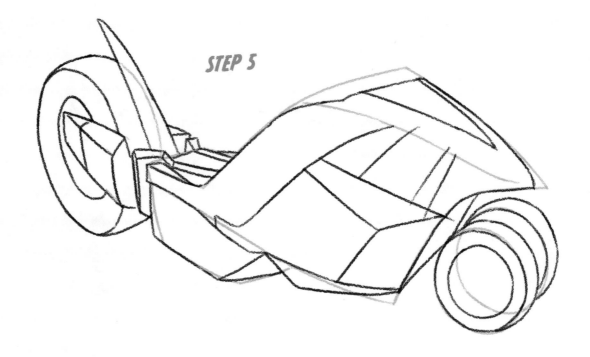

STEP 5

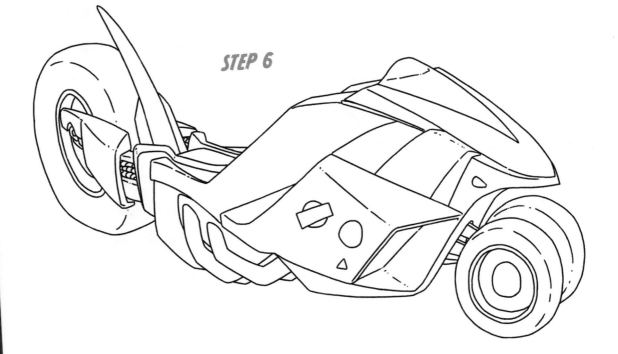

STEP 6

Once your motorcycle is done, draw yourself riding it. Don't forget a helmet!

STEP 7

Tires squeal. Clouds of white smoke rise into the air. In just six seconds, this race car goes from 0 to 250 miles (402 km) per hour. ZOOM! A sloping front end helps reduce drag, the force that pushes against all moving objects and tries to slow them down. Less drag equals more speed.

STEP 1

STEP 2

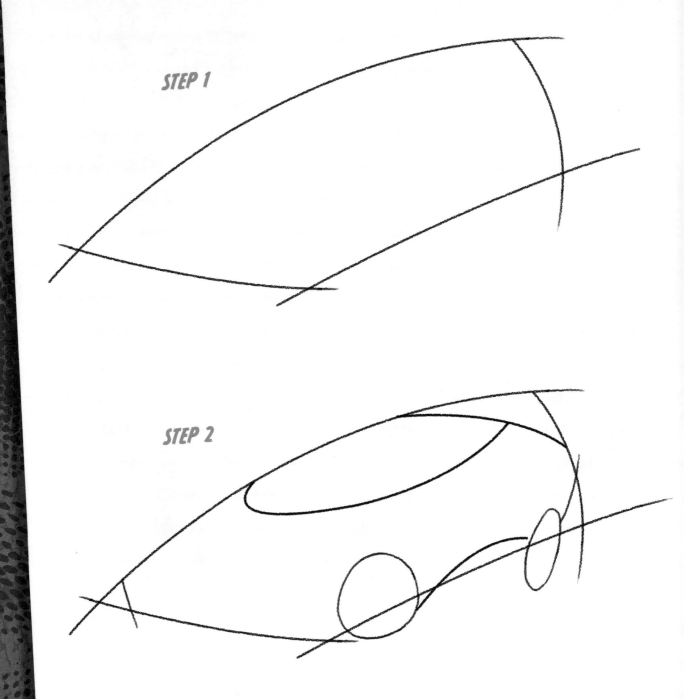

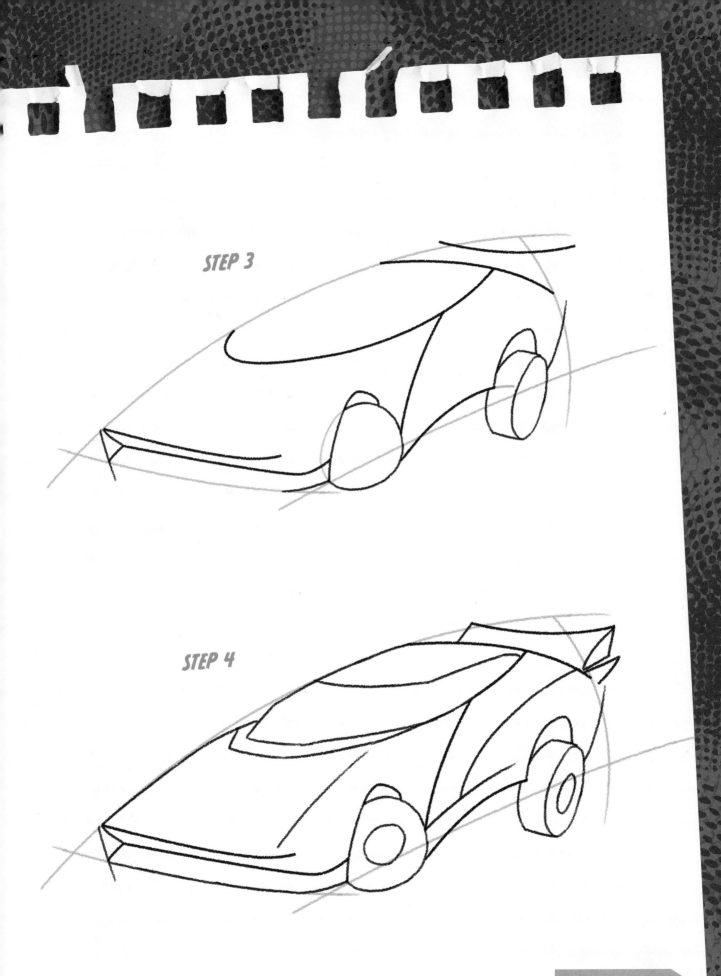

STEP 3

STEP 4

CONTINUED...

STEP 5

STEP 6

It's more fun to race against someone. Draw a few more cars on the track.

STEP 7

OTHER COOL STUFF

WHAT'S COOL TO YOU? Caped heroes saving the day? Battling dinosaurs? Wild animals with razor-sharp teeth and claws? How about the stuff of nightmares, like evil clowns, skeletons, or snake-haired beasts?

This section is stuffed with 25 superhero, dinosaur, animal, and monster projects. They pack a punch and are definitely not for the faint of heart! When you're done drawing them, grab some fresh paper, dig into your imagination, and show the world what cool means to you.

THUNDERFIST

Tired of being small and weak, Carl created a chemical formula to make him strong. Now he's called Thunderfist, and he can rip through concrete like it's cardboard. No crook can hide from this mountain of muscle!

STEP 1

STEP 2

STEP 3

STEP 4

STEP 5

Show off
Thunderfist's
power by drawing
him blasting his
way through a
brick wall.

THE CREATURE

When criminals are on the loose, The Creature goes to work! His snarling face strikes fear into the hearts of criminals far and wide. When he's on the hunt, thugs can't escape his super sense of smell and tireless strength.

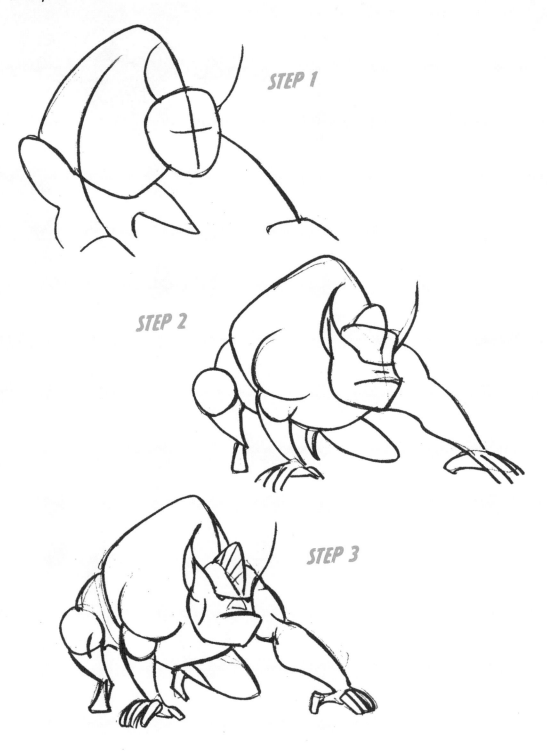

STEP 1

STEP 2

STEP 3

Draw The Creature sniffing out a crook who's hiding behind a tree.

STEP 4

STEP 5

CAPTAIN ATMO

Captain Atmo is the world's most powerful hero. He's more than a mile tall and can pulverize mountains with his sonic fist blast. Whenever giant asteroids or alien ships threaten Earth, Captain Atmo is on the job!

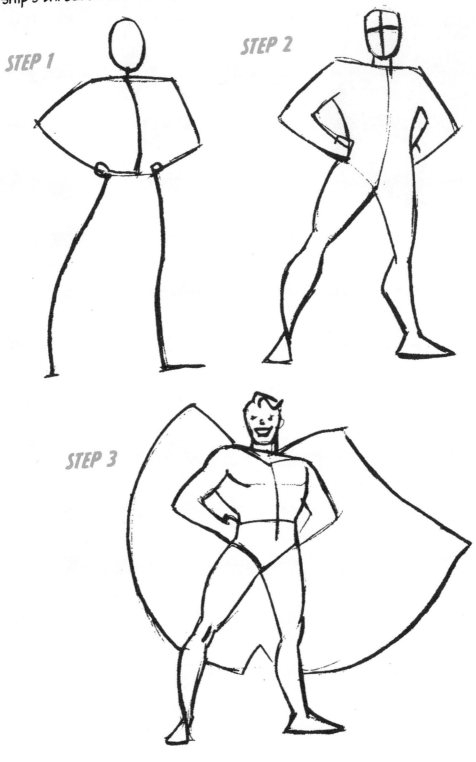

STEP 1

STEP 2

STEP 3

STEP 4

What would Captain Atmo look like as he smashed an asteroid above Earth? Draw him in action!

STEP 5

DRAGONFLY

Joe was just an ordinary pilot who dusted crops for a living—until the day his plane crashed. Joe survived, but he was soaked in chemicals. The next day he woke up with an extra pair of arms, superhuman strength, and he could run at incredible speeds. Now Joe fights crime as the world's newest hero—Dragonfly!

STEP 1

STEP 2

STEP 3

STEP 4

Try drawing Dragonfly chasing down and grabbing some crooks.

STEP 5

TEAM DYNAMO

As a team, the Dynamos have caught hundreds of thieves, muggers, and other thugs. They've also helped put away several major crime bosses. Along with their trusted family pet, Mighty Mutt, this hero team is feared by criminals around the world.

STEP 1

Once you've mastered Team Dynamo, draw them in action! Show them saving the day in some way.

STEP 3

CONTINUED...

STEP 4

STEP 5

STEP 6

STEP 7

GREAT WHITE SHARK

Great white sharks are ferocious predators. They grow to about 16 feet (4.9 m) long. Their mouths often have as many as 3,000 sharp, jagged teeth. You don't want to come face-to-face with one of these huge "wolves of the sea!"

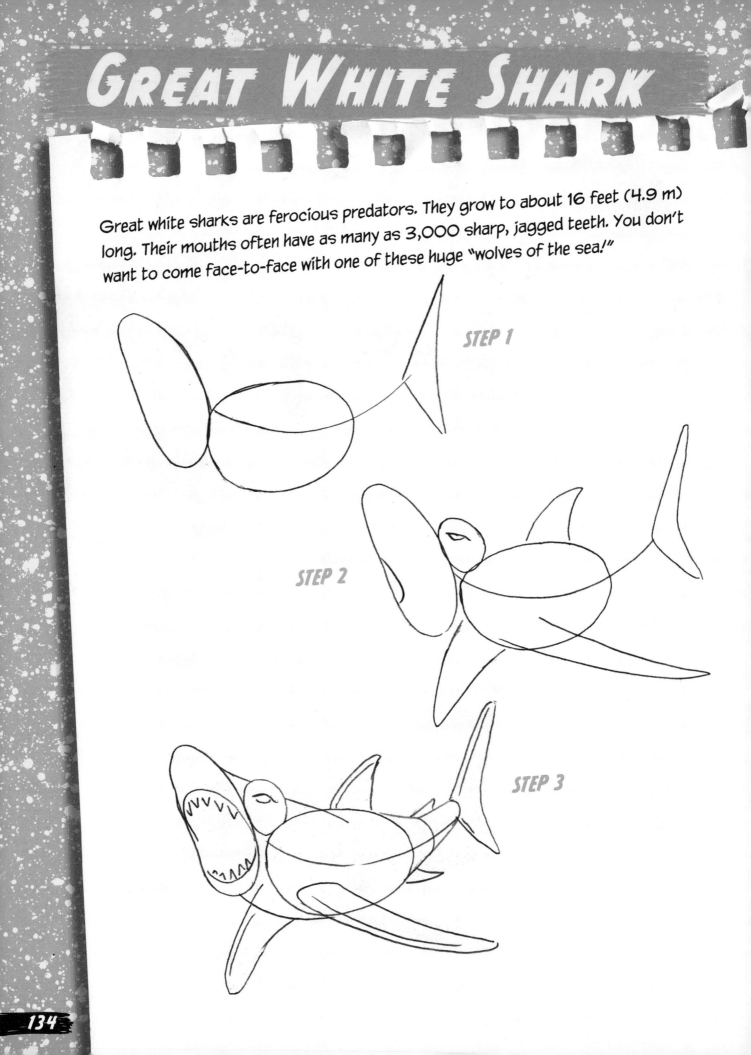

STEP 1

STEP 2

STEP 3

STEP 4

After drawing one shark, draw a bunch more in a feeding frenzy.

STEP 5

HIPPOPOTAMUS

Although a hippopotamus looks friendly, it's best to keep your distance. These massive 4,000-pound (1,814-kilogram) mammals can be very aggressive. And they can run faster than people for short distances. If you see one of these in the wild, be ready to quickly climb a tree!

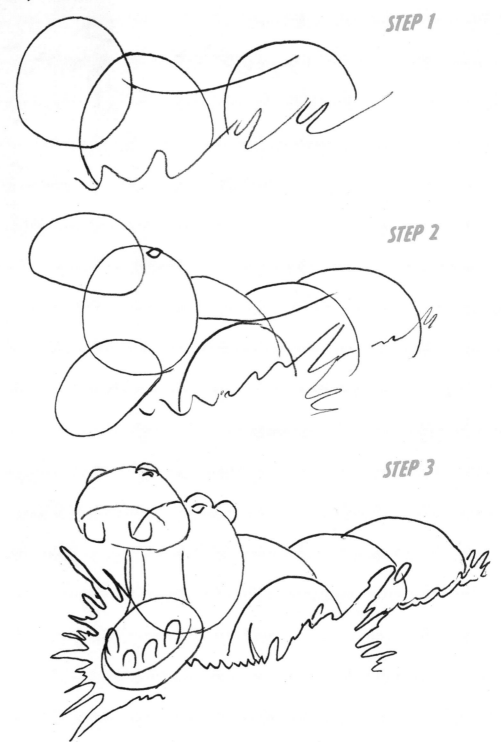

STEP 1

STEP 2

STEP 3

STEP 4

STEP 5

Try drawing a flock of birds being scared off by this hippo's roar.

KOMODO DRAGON

Komodo dragons are the biggest lizards in the world. Their saliva is packed with deadly bacteria. Just one bite can infect and kill prey in just a few days. If you're ever in Indonesia, keep an eye out for these deadly reptiles!

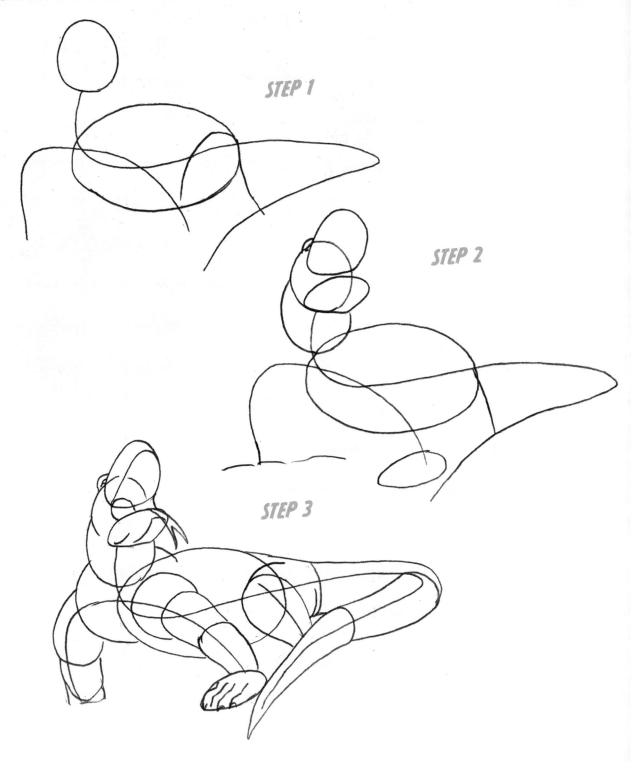

STEP 1

STEP 2

STEP 3

STEP 4

Lunchtime! Show this big lizard swallowing a pig or deer whole.

STEP 5

TIMBER WOLF

Wolves are the ancestors of dogs, but they're not man's best friend. They travel and hunt in packs, so if you see one, there are probably more wolves nearby. There is little to fear, though, because wolves rarely attack people. Just stay back, and they will leave you alone.

STEP 1

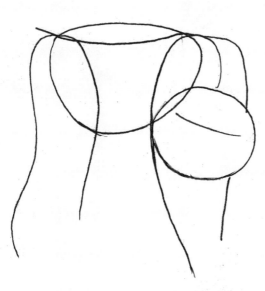

STEP 2

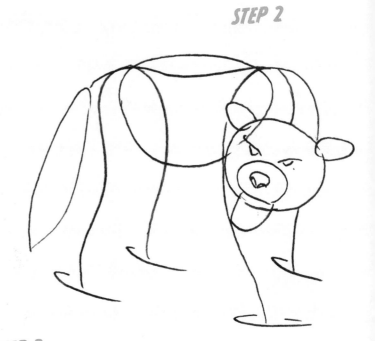

STEP 3

STEP 4

After drawing this wolf, try drawing a pack of them hunting an elk or moose.

STEP 5

BENGAL TIGER

Bengal tigers live mostly in India and Bangladesh. These big cats are fierce predators. Their orange fur and black stripes help them hide in tall grass when hunting prey. They'll eat almost anything—even elephants!

STEP 1

STEP 2

STEP 3

STEP 4

STEP 5

Draw this tiger chasing down a water buffalo.

AFRICAN ELEPHANT

The African elephant is the heaviest land animal on Earth. These giant mammals weigh as much as 7.5 tons (6.8 t). If you see one of these charging at you, there's only one thing you can do—run!

STEP 1

STEP 2

STEP 3

STEP 4

Once you've mastered this elephant, draw a charging herd of them.

STEP 5

SALTWATER CROCODILE

Saltwater crocodiles are the largest reptiles living in the world today. These huge beasts can grow up to 23 feet (7 m) long and weigh more than 3,300 pounds (1,497 kg). Keep away, or it might turn you into a tasty snack!

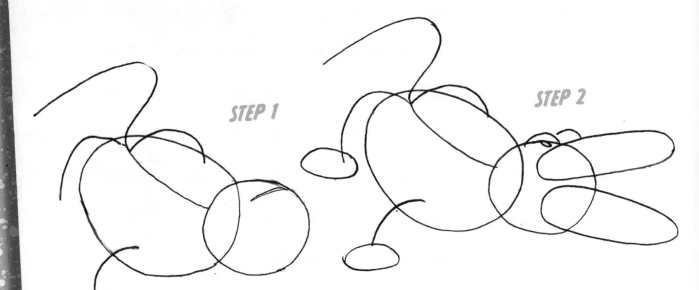

STEP 1

STEP 2

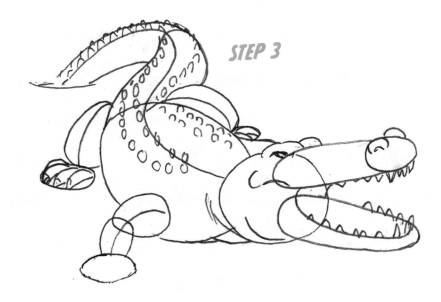

STEP 3

STEP 4

Draw this big beast sinking its teeth into a turtle or wading bird.

STEP 5

T-REX

The T-rex was a vicious hunter. It attacked other dinosaurs by ripping into them with its powerful jaws and huge back claws. Most creatures kept a sharp eye out for this fearsome predator.

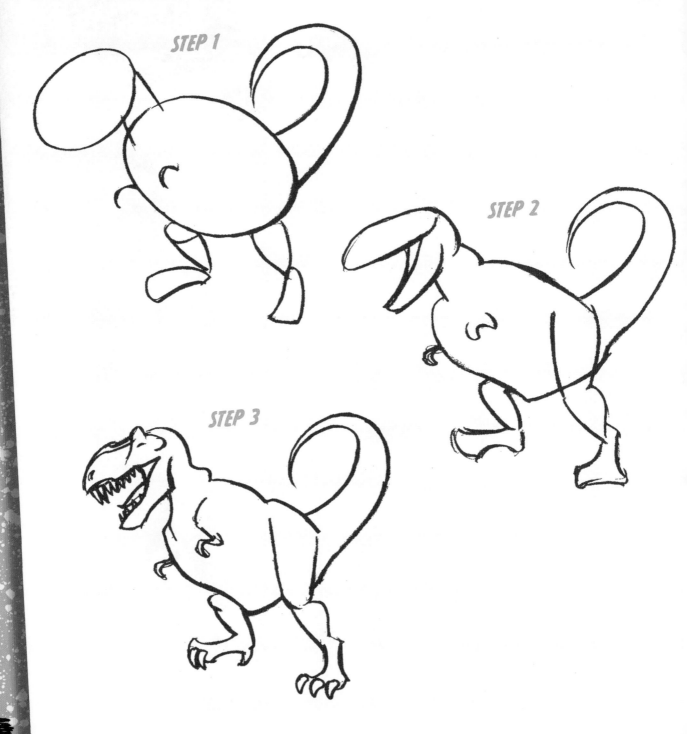

STEP 1

STEP 2

STEP 3

STEP 4

STEP 5

After you've mastered the T–rex, try out the dinosaur fight on page 158.

SPINOSAURUS

Even the mighty T-rex would have a hard fight against the gigantic Spinosaurus. This huge dinosaur was one of the biggest meat-eaters of all time. You definitely don't want this monster coming after you!

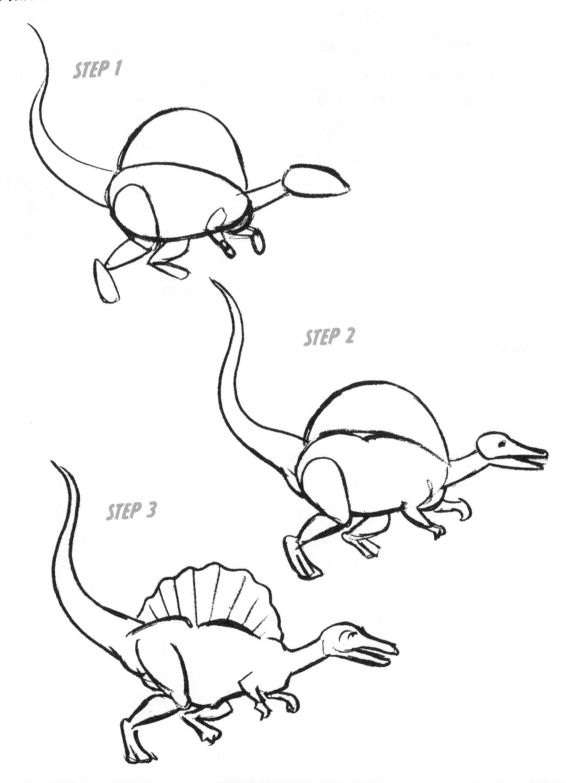

STEP 1

STEP 2

STEP 3

Try drawing this dinosaur in a fight with a T–rex and see who wins.

STEP 4

STEP 5

STEGOSAURUS

Watch out for that tail! Stegosaurus had a wicked defense against predators. Long, sharp spikes on the end of its tail kept enemies at a distance. Large back plates also kept hungry predators from chomping down on this dinosaur.

STEP 1

STEP 2

STEP 3

STEP 4

Give Stegosaurus some nasty battle scars from a fight.

STEP 5

153

TRICERATOPS

If the Triceratops charges, you'd better get out of the way fast! This dinosaur really lived up to its name, which means "three-horned face." It used its three large horns as an effective defense against predators.

STEP 1

STEP 2

STEP 3

Once you've practiced drawing this dinosaur, be sure to try out the dino fight on page 158.

STEP 4

STEP 5

VELOCIRAPTOR

This creature looks strange, but don't be fooled. The Velociraptor was a fast and deadly hunter. It could run up to 40 miles (64 km) per hour. Its wicked claws and needlelike teeth easily tore into its prey.

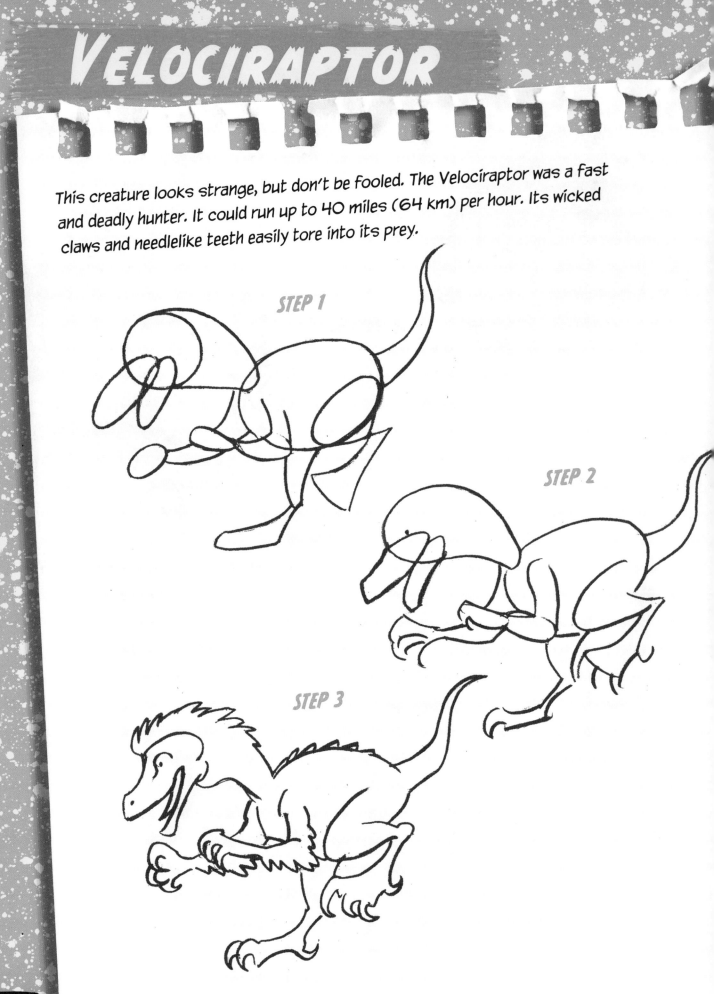

STEP 1

STEP 2

STEP 3

Draw a pack of Velociraptors on the hunt for fresh meat.

STEP 4

STEP 5

DINO FIGHT

Don't get in the middle of this fight! One wrong move and the T-rex might decide that you'd be an easier meal. Or you might have to run from the Triceratops and his three huge horns. Which dino do you think will win?

STEP 1

Once you've mastered this dino fight, try it again with the other dinosaurs from this book.

STEP 2

STEP 3

CONTINUED...

STEP 4

STEP 5

STEP 6

STEP 7

KRACKED KARL

Keep away from Kracked Karl the Krazy Klown! He was a simple circus clown who just wanted to make people laugh. But nobody thought he was funny. Now his mission is to make you laugh at his jokes—or else!

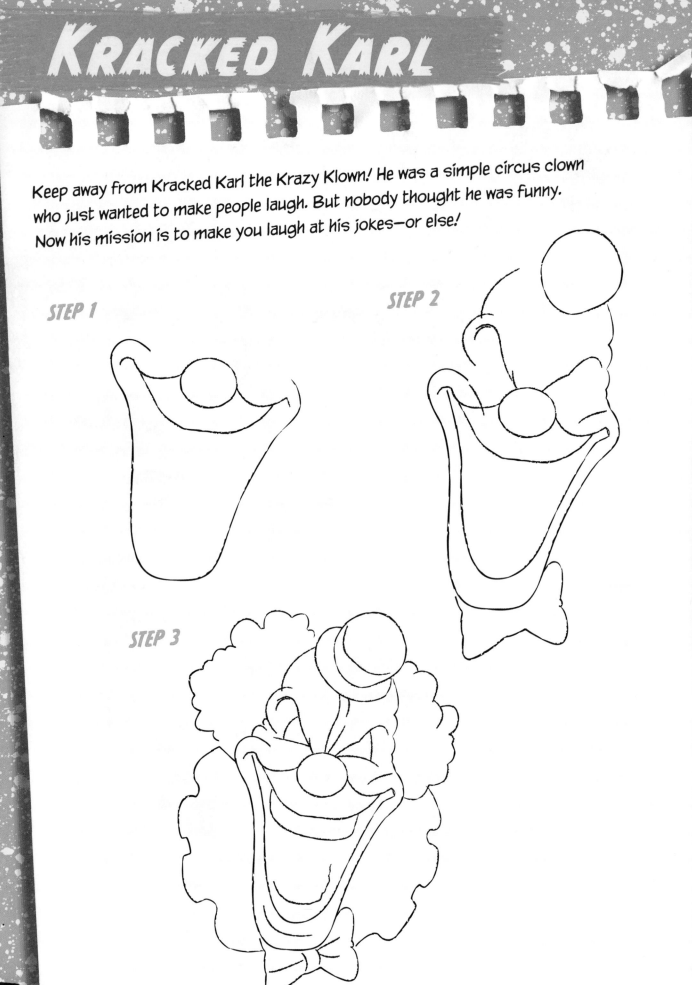

STEP 1

STEP 2

STEP 3

STEP 4

After drawing Karl, try giving him a crazy clown suit and some wacky balloons.

STEP 5

MEDUSA

Medusa was once a beautiful woman. Every man adored her. But the Greek goddess Athena was jealous. She stole Medusa's beauty and changed her hair into hissing snakes. Afterward, any man who looked at Medusa was turned to stone!

STEP 1

STEP 2

STEP 3

STEP 4

Does Medusa have the body of a woman? A snake? Or something in between? Draw it!

STEP 5

SKELETAL SOLDIER

Even the bravest warriors tremble in fear when facing an army of skeletal soldiers! These undead creatures do not fear death. And they never stop fighting until their bones are smashed to bits.

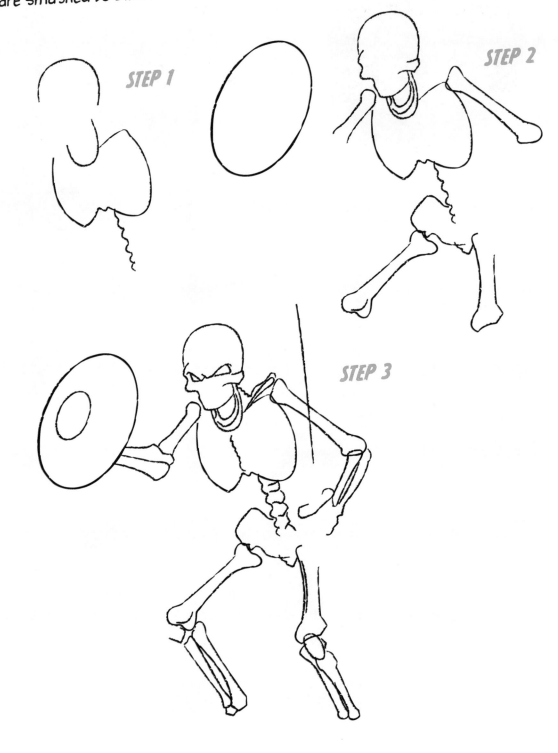

STEP 1

STEP 2

STEP 3

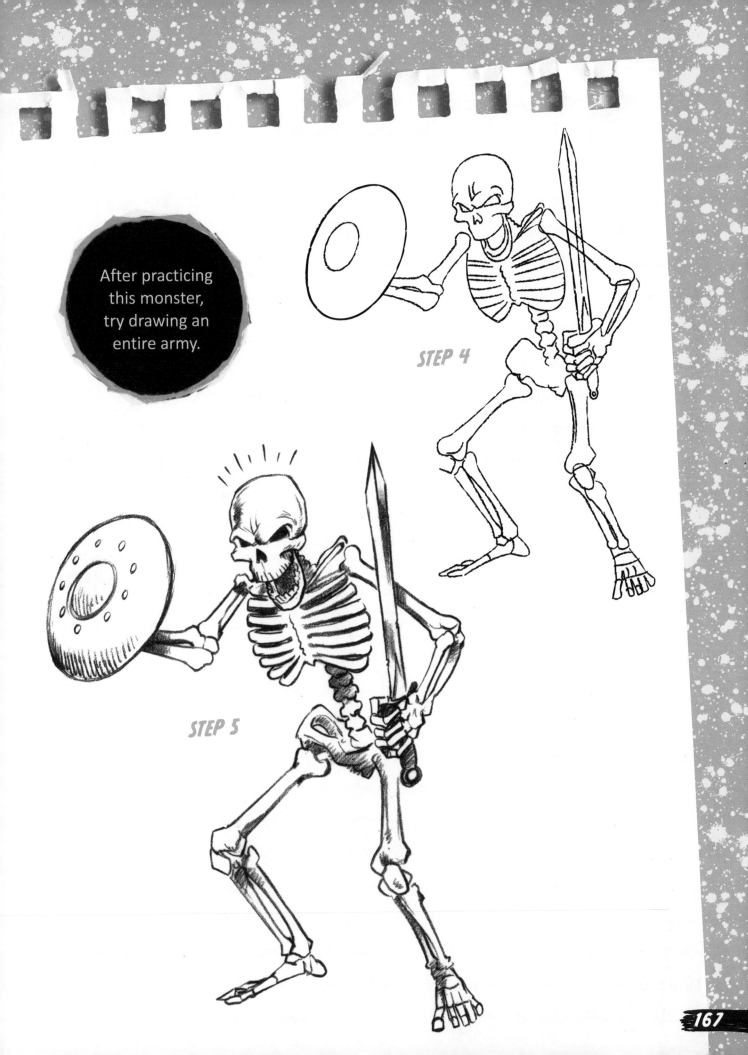

After practicing this monster, try drawing an entire army.

STEP 4

STEP 5

FRANK STEIN

Poor Frank Stein. He just wants to be everyone's friend. But people keep chasing him with pitchforks and torches. It's just not easy being super tall, with green skin and bolts sticking out of your head!

STEP 1

STEP 2

STEP 3

STEP 4

Make Frank smile! Draw him dancing with his monster wife.

STEP 5

KING HOTEP

Who dares to disturb King Hotep's sleep? Watch out, this is one mad mummy! Even after a 3,000-year nap, Hotep still wakes up cranky. Quick, give him a glass of warm milk. Otherwise he might take you on a permanent vacation—to his tomb!

STEP 1

STEP 2

STEP 3

STEP 4

STEP 5

Try drawing a happy mummy sitting at a table with some milk and cookies.

FISHY PHIL

Fishy Phil is a gruesome monster from the deep oceans. His huge eyes help him see in the dark depths. He easily catches prey with his sharp claws. Phil is also an excellent swimmer. You'd better run if you see his scaly head pop out of the water!

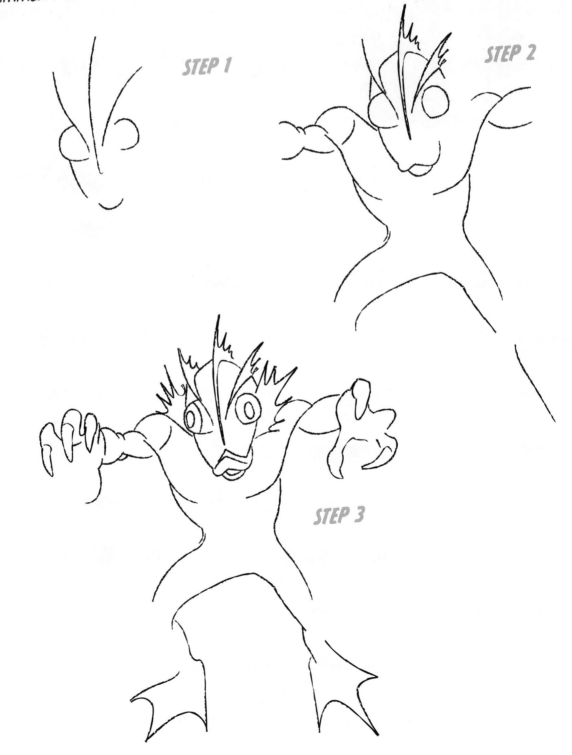

STEP 1

STEP 2

STEP 3

Draw Phil swimming in the ocean with schools of tiny fish.

STEP 4

STEP 5

UGH THE THUG

Ugh is a simple troll. It doesn't take much to make him happy. He loves to catch weary travelers crossing his bridge. Usually, he'll just take all their gold. But sometimes, he'll cook them for his dinner!

STEP 1

STEP 2

STEP 3

STEP 4

Try drawing Ugh in a tug-of-war with his brother, Chugh, over a bag of stolen gold.

STEP 5

SHIRE BRIDGE PAY R T¹OLL

Published by Capstone Press, 1710 Roe Crest
Drive, North Mankato, Minnesota, 56003

www.mycapstone.com

Library of Congress Cataloging-in-Publication
data is available on the Library of Congress
website.

ISBN: 978-1-5435-1562-6

Summary: Basic, step-by-step instructions
teach beginning artists how to draw more than
70 projects of particular interest to boys,
including aliens, robots, vehicles, and more.

Designers: Aruna Rangarajan and Kyle Grenz

Image Credits: Shutterstock: all backgrounds,
Jamen Percy, 5 (color pencils and scribbles),
Lifestyle Graphic (sheet of paper), 6 and
throughout, Mega Pixel, 5 (erasers and pencil
sharpener), Ruslan Ivantsov, 5 (graphite
pencil), Sanit Fuangnakhon, cover (pencil),
timquo, 5 (felt marker)